M000213780

THE FIRST SUPER APP

INSIDE CHINA'S WECHAT AND THE NEW DIGITAL REVOLUTION

Kevin Shimota

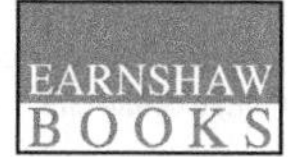

The First Superapp

Kevin Shimota

ISBN-13: 978-988-8769-42-1

COMPUTERS / Electronic Commerce

EB163

Published by Earnshaw Books Ltd. (Hong Kong)

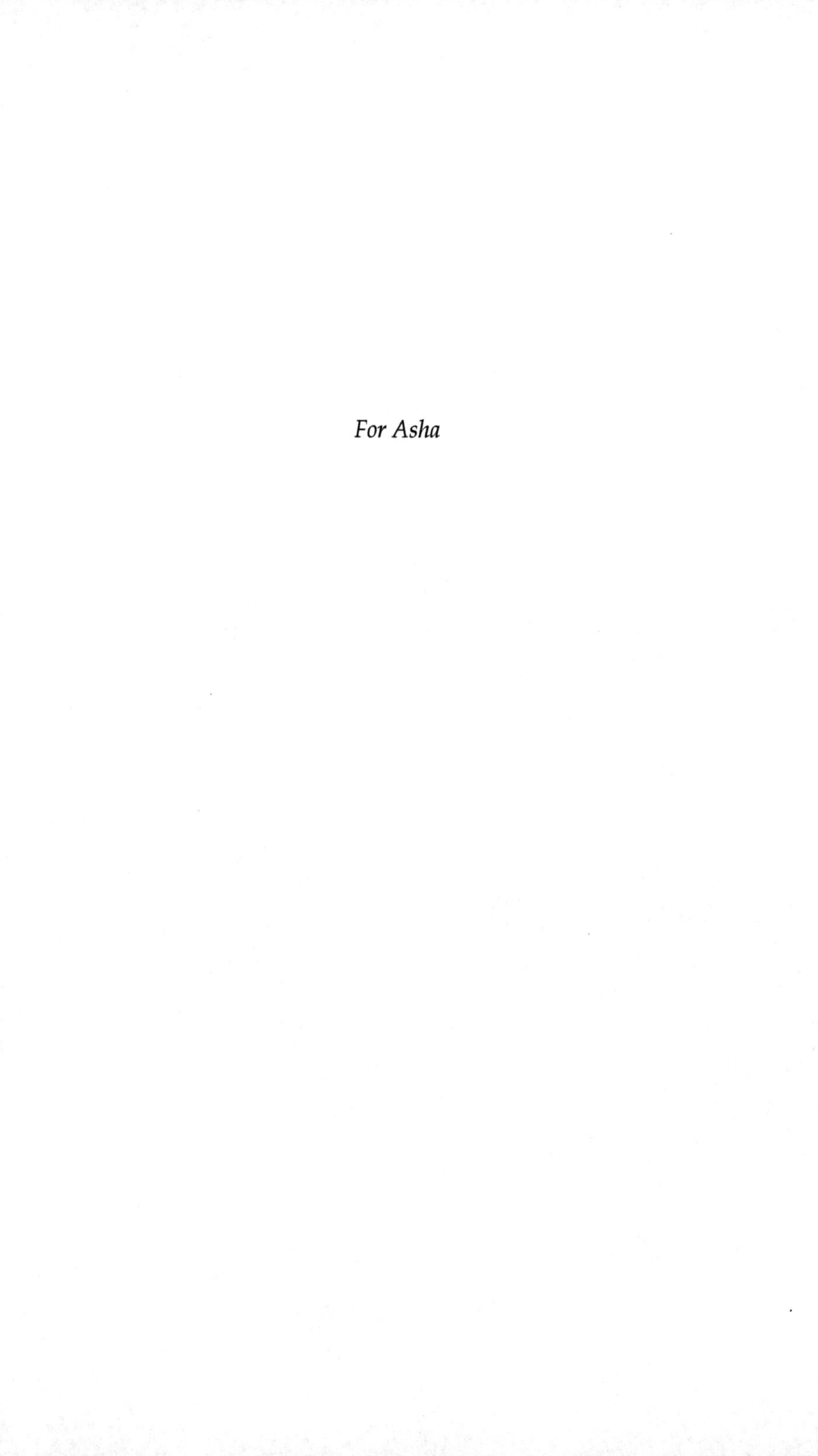

For Asha

Contents

Introduction 1

Chapter 1: Setting the stage 3

Part 1: Creating China's Unique Internet 11
Chapter 2: Understanding the Chinese Internet 13
Tencent vs. Facebook 15
WeChat vs. Facebook 17
Chapter 3: The Chinese Internet and WeChat 22
Splinternets 24
Chapter 4: A Tale of Two Internets 31
Chapter 5: Language 35
Chapter 6: Culture: History, Celebration, and Belief 38
China's History of Isolation 38
Chapter 7: Government 42
The CPC's Approach to the Internet 44
Chapter 8: Scale 48
Chapter 9: Internet Diversity in the Real World 52
Geographic - West and East 52
Industry Case – Ride-hailing Apps 54
Part 2: The WeChat Story 57
Chapter 10: Creation 59
Tencent 59
Chapter 11: Growth 70
The Voice Message Function 71
Connecting Strangers 73

Completing the Social Ecosystem 76
Chapter 12: Connecting Business 80
User Value 80
Monetization 83
Chapter 13: Payment 86
Red Packets 86
QR Code Payment 89
Official Account Payment 90
Chapter 14: Mini Programs 93
The Efficiency Challenge 93
The Mini Program Solution 94
Challenges to Success 98
Mini Games 99
Chapter 15: Recent Trends and Direction 101

Part 3: The Payment-led Digital Revolution 105
Chapter 16: Mobile Payment and Closed-Loop Systems 107
Enhancing Closed-Loop Systems 109
China's Mobile Payment Phenomenon 110
Chapter 17: China's Mobile Payment Explosion 111
Historical: The Two 111
Cultural: Convenience is King 113
Government: Centralized Incentives 114
Businesses: A Story of Two Giants 115
Chapter 18: The Future of Mobile Payment 121
New Tech in China 122
China Going Global 123
Cross-Border Payment 124
International Pay 124
Inbound Tourism 125
Future of Mobile Payments: WeChat Pay vs. Alipay 125
Future of Payment Worldwide 128

Part 4: Superapps 133
Chapter 19: Defining 'Superapp' 135
Users 137
Content 139
Interaction Tools 140
Platform Perspective 141
Chapter 20: Superapp Success Factors 146
Leverage Platform Strategy 146
User-Focused 149
High Frequency 149
Positioning 152
Iterative 153
Architecture – Lowering barriers to entry 154
User Design 156
Governance 157
Smart Monetization 158
Chapter 21: The Good and the Bad of Superapps 160
Benefits 160
Costs and Challenges 164
Chapter 22: Joining Superapps 166
Hospitality – Starbucks 166
Tourism – CityExperience 176
Attractions – Burj Khalifa 183
Entertainment – Merlin Entertainment 185
Chapter 23: Conclusion 188

Bibliography 191

Introduction

How did China, a country that was a technological backwater until just a few decades ago, become the modern wonder that it is today? After centuries of isolation, how did it transform its people and economy to become a significant player on the world stage? How and why did it develop its own internet, distinct and in many ways separate from the World Wide Web used by most of the world, but every bit as sophisticated and efficient? And how did China develop the first digital Superapp that was selectively designed to both enhance the lives of individual Chinese and be a significant factor in the growth of the Chinese economy?

I have had ample opportunity to observe this transformation and become familiar with the process used by one of China's largest technology companies, Tencent. For four years, I worked at the epicenter of China's tech world. Educated in China and fluent in Mandarin, I was one of the only foreigners working at WeChat, a Tencent subsidiary whose single product became the world's first Superapp. Heading up global efforts, I worked closely with company leaders, including founder Allen Zhang, and was privy to WeChat's behind-the-scenes strategy. I observed as a Westerner and participated as an insider, which afforded a unique understanding of the new China and its place in the world.

To share this broader story, I have taken my singular experiences working at WeChat to provide insight into Chinese business philosophy in the 21st century. First, by studying the genesis and evolution of the product, you will see how history and culture have contributed to this most revolutionary digital creation. Second, you will gain an understanding of China's internet by experiencing it through the lens of WeChat and how the internet's design and implementation foster the economic, social, and political advancement of China. Third, you will better understand what to expect as China expands its role on the global stage. Lastly, you will share my sense of how Chinese technology influences the global economy and better understand the barriers that limit international business in China and the challenges Chinese tech faces in the worldwide market.

1

Setting the Stage

In 1978, China began to institute a program of market reform, trade liberalization, and enhanced opportunity, opening the country to foreign trade and investment and rapidly advancing a relatively isolated nation to the global stage. As a result, China became one of the world's fastest-growing markets, averaging annual economic growth consistently approaching double digits through 2018 and lifting more than 850 million people out of poverty. Although the growth rate has leveled off to a healthy 5-6%, China has continued to expand its economy worldwide. China's transformation from a backwater in East Asia to a superpower at the forefront of global affairs has transferred both capital and power to China, creating a paradigm shift that has had ripple effects in business, politics, and technology across the globe.

While significantly enhancing the quality of life across China, this economic miracle has also created tensions between China and other leading economic powers. The Western media view China in terms of headline stories and focus on controversial issues, such as the situation of Hong Kong, digital security and Huawei, the status of human rights, and the position of minorities. However, within China, people experience a very different reality. They live behind the – literally and figuratively – Great Firewall of China. They see the Chinese side of these issues as disseminated by the Chinese government through an increasingly digital and interwoven system. Government messaging emphasizes the importance of thriving in a flourishing and stable economy, disregards isolation from global networks, and renders the topics of Western concerns essentially irrelevant or non-existent.

As we will see, the political differences between China and Western nations are a significant factor in the historic reticence of China to open its markets and the reluctance of Western businesses to acknowledge the validity of Chinese trade and technology. From the Western perspective, China as a communist country is viewed with some suspicion. However, the successes of the government and China's economic transformation are self-evident, and they are inextricably bound together. In many ways, the two reinforce one another.

While no equivalent Western nations have a Communist political system, understanding the differences imposed on China is essential to understanding China's digital revolution and developing a dialogue among global business communities. This is important because with a 70% internet penetration rate, well above the world's average, China is highly digital. (The World Bank, n.d.) In fact, China has the most internet users of any country. This connectivity permits individuals to do business, communicate, and access entertainment in new ways. Moreover, China has embraced smartphones to an extent unseen anywhere else in the world, creating a digital environment that is the heart of modern China. To better understand the degree of digital engagement in modern China, consider the following everyday scenarios:

- In a street market in Chongqing, a man buys some fresh Szechuan chili peppers from a merchant. He asks for a kilo, and she hands him a massive bag of chilis and says, "30 yuan" (about US$4), nodding toward a Quick Response (QR) code dangling from a string above her stall. He scans the code with the WeChat app on his phone – more on WeChat shortly – inputs the amount, and hits pay. Finally, he leaves with his peppers, excited to enjoy a spicy meal. Meanwhile, the merchant realizes she is running out of peppers. Maybe it's the cold weather? So she uses WeChat to message her supplier to add another 10 kilograms to tomorrow's delivery.

- In a restaurant in Guangzhou, four working-class friends are getting together for a hotpot dinner. One of them scans the QR code on the table with WeChat. This opens a WeChat mini program with a restaurant menu. After consulting his friends, he selects several items and pays for the food. Moments later, their meal arrives. While they wait, one of the diners notices his phone battery is low and uses WeChat to rent a portable battery from the battery rental station on the restaurant counter. He uses it to charge his phone. After the meal, the man who ordered and paid the bill uses WeChat to send a "split the bill" link and, just by tapping the link, the other friends pay their portions.
- In a shopping mall, a couple is out on a date. They see a karaoke booth, which looks like a giant telephone box. The woman uses WeChat to scan the QR code on the control panel and pays 20 yuan (US$3) for four songs. As they finish, the booth automatically sends the woman's WeChat recordings of their performances, accompanied by reports of their vocal

accuracy. She starts to forward them to his mother. He, far too embarrassed, laughs and quickly stops her.

- A man riding home in a taxi is responding to WeChat messages from work colleagues. He remembers that he hasn't paid his water bill, so he opens WeChat Pay and pays both his water and electricity bills in seconds. As he leaves the taxi at the front of his apartment, WeChat Pay automatically pays his fare. It notifies him of the exact amount paid. He goes to the parcel delivery box for his apartment complex and scans the central console with his WeChat. One of the lockers automatically opens. The phone charging cable he ordered that afternoon using WeChat has already arrived. He grabs the small parcel and heads inside.

WeChat, the application used in all these scenarios, is at the center of the digital revolution and provides a striking illustration of the transformation of Chinese society through digitization. It began as a simple messaging app and is now all-encompassing. It provides access to everything that enhances and facilitates day-to-day living. Chinese people chat, call, read, learn, play, and pay bills on WeChat. It is available from marketplaces to apartment complexes and in rural and urban environments. Effectively, WeChat is China's WhatsApp, Facebook, Instagram, Twitter, Amazon, PayPal, and much more, consolidated into a single interface. Virtually anything you'd want to do with a smartphone can be accomplished via this Superapp.

It is a Superapp which is nearly unknown outside of China, consolidating hundreds of multiple services, including tools like payments and mini operating systems, into one single universally available mobile application. The true measure of a Superapp is that you don't need other apps, you just need the one, effectively being able to replace every other app on your phone, and then on top of that, providing new value that you didn't have before. WeChat easily accomplishes this - it is integral to modern life in China. Chinese people might be able to live without their smartphone but they cannot live without WeChat.

WeChat was the first app to reach Superapp status; the term was popularized to explain the app's unprecedented success. While many upstarts and mature products contend to reach a similar Superapp status, WeChat easily remains the most dominant and quintessential Superapp to this day.

WeChat's success has triggered several other hyper-functional apps in an evolving digital revolution.. Although the West for many years viewed these and other digital products, including WeChat, as Chinese oddities and copycats of more highly developed Western products, it is becoming increasingly difficult for the West to dismiss the success of these products. Western entrepreneurs, including Facebook's founder, Mark Zuckerberg, have recognized the opportunities and information to be gleaned from studying China's innovations. Zuckerbreg recently announced that Facebook will begin a strategic transformation to emulate WeChat. (Yuan, 2018)

WeChat and its cohorts do far more than make life easier for the average Chinese person, they are changing China's economic landscape. In 2016, China already boasted a whopping US$9 trillion in mobile payment transactions, dwarfing the United States' US$112 billion by a factor of 80. (Purnell, 2017) Since then, the gap has continued to widen. Chinese people no longer use physical wallets or carry cash and credit cards. This has created an all-new business environment, giving rise to many ideas from coconut vending machines to the stationless bike-share boom.

The Chinese internet is the foundation of China's digital revolution. The explosion of Superapps and successful digital products would not be possible without the internet environment that China has created. While many governments have control of their nation's internet services, the Chinese government's scale of internet control is unparalleled. The government has created a "walled garden" in which local Chinese tech companies flourish. However, the forces that enhance China's productivity and quality of life also hinder Chinese companies from expanding globally. Understanding China's unique internet is critical to understanding China's modern digital revolution and future global trends originating from China.

How did this happen? How did WeChat, a simple messaging application, become the world's first Superapp and achieve nearly total market penetration in China? How did this unique internet and the applications it supports surpass the West in critical categories, such as mobile finance?

During my tenure with WeChat, I led partnerships with other divisions across Tencent. In addition, I liaised with prominent international brands, such as Starbucks, Burberry, and the Burj Khalifa. The issue for companies doing business in China was, and still is, that international brands want to be part of the massive Chinese market, but to do so, they must modify their business models to fit the country's unique environment. To modify their models, they must first understand China's digital ecosystem, how and why it was developed, how it is enabled by the government and reinforces the government point of view, and how it is influencing the world. This is key to understanding China's modern state, landscape, and direction.

I've organized this book into four parts: first, the environment and the social context that produced China's internet; second, WeChat's story from start-up to Superapp; third, WeChat's contribution to China's payment-led digital revolution; fourth, examining the new Superapp phenomenon and how to make or join one.

Part 1

Creating China's Unique Internet

Part 1 examines how the internet is no longer a singular technology – China's internet is vastly different from that of the rest of the world. Four contextual factors contribute to this distinct implementation: language, culture, government, and scale. Exploring this context enables us to understand how and why the country developed its own unique internet, which gave birth to the first Superapp.

2

Understanding the Chinese Internet

The internet of China looks very different from the World Wide Web which people in most parts of the world use. For one thing, there are thousands of online products and platforms that are rarely seen outside China and the Chinese diaspora. These include Tencent, Alibaba, WeChat, Taobao, Alipay, JD.com , TikTok, QQ, Renren, Weibo, Douban, Dazhong Dianping, Huawei, Xiaomi, Didi, Zhihu, Mobike, Himalaya radio, and more. The services provided by these products, all of which are accessed through the internet, range from hailing a cab to booking a cleaning service.

Within Western nations, a common approach to understanding the complexity of the Chinese internet is to use the 'anchoring' comparison, which describes a direct relationship between Western products and their Chinese equivalents. In this scenario, Baidu is Google, Alibaba is Amazon, and Tencent is Facebook. WeChat is the equivalent of Whatsapp, Weibo is China's Twitter, Dazhong Dianping is Yelp, Xiaomi strives to be China's Apple, and Huawei is China's Cisco. However, anchoring can only partially describe China's digital phenomena because this type of comparison vastly oversimplifies the features and functionality of Chinese technology.

For example, Alibaba references modern-day Amazon, but when it began, it was much more similar to eBay. In fact, when entering the Chinese market, eBay actively courted Alibaba, but

Alibaba wouldn't be bought out, Alibaba's founder Jack Ma had too many dreams and ambitions, and eBay bought a competing Chinese ecommerce platform. Then began a fierce battle for China's ecommerce market which Alibaba won by offering financial incentives and creating an appealing internet presence that catered to the Chinese mindset. The development of Alibaba's comprehensive payment tool, Alipay, which is similar to eBay's PayPal, was Alibaba's most distinguishing feature and major contributor to its immediate success. At this time, the incorporation of a financial component continues to distinguish Alibaba from Amazon and others. Amazon's own similar tool, Amazon Pay, has barely reached beyond payments for Amazon.com services but continues to evolve.

Similarly, Huawei was a near replica of Cisco. Both manufactured software and hardware for network information systems. However, unlike Cisco, which remained in the Business-to-Business (B2B) and Business-to-Government (B2G) categories,

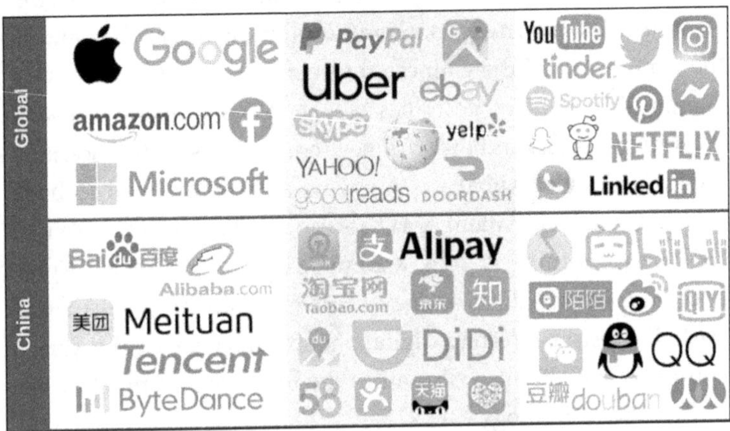

Figure 1: The Internet of China vs. Global.

Chinese users see a very different internet ecosystem than the rest of the world. Many products and companies mirror the West but with their own Chinese flavors, while some Chinese products have no Western equivalents.

Huawei took deliberate steps into the Business-to-Consumer (B2C) and Consumer-to-Consumer (C2C) world of smartphones. As a result, Huawei would briefly become the world's largest smartphone seller before hitting major road bumps when a combination of sanctions and a global backlash limited its international expansion.

Tencent is one of the largest Chinese technology firms but also one of the least known and understood. Tencent has been described as comparable to Facebook, but its products, QQ and WeChat, bear little resemblance to their Facebook counterparts, Messenger and Whatsapp. Furthermore, Tencent's core strategies of utilizing Games for monetization and focusing on tools, such as mobile payment using WeChat Pay, truly set the platform apart from Facebook. To better understand the evolution of Chinese digital technology and how and why it differs so dramatically from Western tech, it is helpful to examine the development and evolution of Tencent and Facebook. Note that Facebook has changed its name to 'Meta,' but I'll refer to the company as 'Facebook' for simplicity.

Tencent vs. Facebook

Both Tencent and Facebook focus on the social and community aspect of peoples' lives. Their core value is in facilitating human interaction. Their ecosystems are based on redirecting and refocusing the traffic created by people as they access their platforms for business or pleasure. In both instances, redirection is how these platforms monetize. However, they accomplish this strategy very differently. For example, 98% of Facebook's revenue derives from advertisements, in stark contrast with Tencent's 17%. These underlying differences between Facebook and Tencent reflect the differences between Chinese and Western digital technology development and introduces the various financial technology (fintech) strategies that distinguish Chinese from Western technologies.

Tencent has more than 180 products, which offer a broad range of services, including games; desktop messaging platforms like QQ; a video streaming platform, Tencent video; and a music streaming platform called QQ music. Tencent's monetization comes from several of these products, as no single product provides more than a sixth of its total revenue.

Facebook, on the other hand, has very few products that generate revenue. The most significant monetizer is the Facebook platform. In 2020, 60% of Facebook's revenue came directly from the Facebook platform. To diversify, Facebook has purchased other products to expand its ecosystem, including Whatsapp and Instagram. Whatsapp isn't a significant monetizer, but Instagram accounted for more than 30% of Facebook's revenue in 2020, up from 13.2% in 2016. (Facebook, Inc, 2020)

Tencent diversifies monetization across various product categories, with the three most successful monetization categories being games, fintech services, and advertising. In 2020, these accounted for 39%, 27%, and 17% of total revenue, respectively. Tencent's monetization strategy is to focus on "value-added services." In this paradigm, consumers purchase games, in-game goods, digital tools, and subscriptions for entertainment, as needed within the Tencent ecosystem. As a result, the Tencent strategy focuses monetization efforts on these services. In doing so, advertising revenue is minimized to less than 20% of total revenues. (Tencent, Inc., 2020)

In 2020, 98% of Facebook's revenue came from advertisements. This may be because Facebook only owns social media products, which limits its monetizing methods, or it may be that Facebook has no interest in diversifying its revenue model. Either way, Facebook's revenue model is significantly more unitary than

Tencent's. This difference in their monetization models produces two very different user experiences. For example, a WeChat user sees a maximum of three ads on Moments – similar to Facebook's Wall – each day. In contrast, a Facebook user's exposure is unlimited and could be in the hundreds or even thousands of ads during a session.

The point of this comparison is not to suggest that one platform is better than the other. Instead, it demonstrates that, while the two companies are both social media platforms, their ecosystems are incredibly different. For this reason, it is unproductive to compare the parent companies, Tencent and Facebook, directly. However, an examination of the primary applications of each, Facebook and the Tencent product, WeChat, provides some interesting insights.

WeChat vs. Facebook

Both the differences and similarities of WeChat and Facebook originate in their unique evolutionary paths. At the macro level, WeChat facilitates a more closed, private, and individual user experience, while Facebook champions an open, social, and highly visible user presence.

Facebook was created in 2004, well before smartphones or tablets were commonplace, when the personal computer (PC) was the sole internet access tool. During product development, Facebook optimized its functionality, user experience, and systems for personal computers running web-browsers. This cemented the relationship between the Facebook product and the personal computer, such that the PC user interface and product strategies appropriate to the PC were an intrinsic component of Facebook's DNA.

In the early 2000s, as smartphones began to gain traction as operating platforms, they were supported by improved batteries, miniaturization, and faster digital data networks, which facilitated their expanded functionality. When Apple released the first iPhone in 2007, the era of the digital smartphone and mobile device truly began. Many companies and products that had dominated during the PC era struggled to adapt to the emergence of the smartphone. Facebook was among those companies facing the challenges and opportunities that the smartphone enabled. To address the issue, Facebook closed its doors for three months. They rethought all aspects of the product, from back-end code to the user interface, to meet the goal of adapting to the mobile era. This was a problematic transformation that required massive resources and manpower. Rather than retool from the beginning, Facebook chose to modify its existing product. As a result, Facebook's DNA was not entirely transformed, and it retains significant baggage from the desktop era. That said, many experts believe that Facebook's rebirth as both a smartphone and PC application was one of the more successful transformations in Silicon Valley. This was clearly reflected in its stock performance.

In contrast, WeChat was developed as a mobile application from the beginning and, as such, avoided the challenge of moving from the desktop to the mobile device. Tencent had an existing desktop messenger application called QQ but was concerned that QQ was too slow to perform well on a mobile device. To meet this challenge, WeChat was created as a totally new smartphone app.

Beginning as a mobile application had many benefits. The user interface was optimized for smartphone usage. The user experience was smooth and stable across the smartphone universe with few bugs. Users were identified and verified by using each individual's existing phone number. As an application built expressly for the mobile environment, WeChat's DNA was and continues to be better adapted to the smartphone era.

WeChat is a mobile application and a closed system by default. While the mobile vs. desktop DNA distinction does not directly impact the open vs. closed dichotomy, mobile applications lend themselves to tight packaging within closed server environments, while internet-based programs on PCs are publicly available, searchable, and easily read. Content is available within the application itself, but that content is not searchable on the World Wide Web. Because WeChat content does not appear on a Baidu search, only defined friends can see shared content or identify individuals within group chats. Facebook, on the other hand, is an open system based on World Wide Web principles. By default, content that individuals share can be seen by friends of friends and the general public.

Another example of the closed vs. open distinction is how friends are added on the two different platforms. WeChat prioritizes adding friends they meet in-person or have intimate knowledge of their details. Most people simply add WeChat friends during face-to-face interactions by scanning the other person's QR code. Adding an individual without a QR scan requires inputting their exact WeChat ID or associated phone number. By contrast, Facebook allows users to add friends by entering a name or sufficient information to identify an individual profile. The user simply searches the name and can see the resulting profiles of people the user has probably never met. This means a user can peruse any account of anyone anywhere in the world without having actually met the person. Facebook provides Friend suggestions using a newsfeed; Facebook's algorithm makes guesses about people you are meeting, have met, or, in the opinion of the algorithm, should meet in your day-to-day life. These product aspects are based on an open concept with the goal of broadening a user's number of social contacts, which is advantageous for revenue acquisition through advertising but may have negative implications for user privacy. Closed systems, such as WeChat, make Friend requests from unknown individuals a rare occurrence.

Facebook began as a social networking system (SNS) platform with its core product feature, the Facebook Wall. Users share their happenings with all of their friends by posting on the Wall, which invites viewers to respond to the Wall posting. This feature was the initial Facebook-designed communication method. SNS is more of a bulletin board for the masses than direct messaging to specific people. Facebook's messaging functionality wouldn't evolve until years later and eventually would spin-off to become a separate Facebook integrated application, Messenger. Today, Messenger has staggering user numbers, around 1.3 billion people using the app monthly. (Kemp, 2021) Although many people complain about a poor user experience, large numbers use Messenger because they already use Facebook. Messenger provides instant access to a user's Facebook community. Its success is attributable to 'positive network externality', when a sufficient number of people use an application, similar users will be incentivized to use it as well.

Conversely, WeChat began as a messaging platform and later added SNS features. While WeChat has successfully integrated SNS into its product features, direct messaging is still its core competence. Today, WeChat is potentially the world's most successful case of combining SNS and messaging with 780 million users a day accessing the SNS feature, called "Moments" or 朋友圈, which is similar to Facebook's Wall but with plenty of Chinese characteristics such as increased privacy and prioritization of immediate friends. (Zhang, 2021)

WeChat messaging is a direct form of communication between an individual and a recipient or group, which may have a maximum of 500 members. WeChat users are more likely than users of other chat applications to create and discuss in large groups of 100 or more. However, regardless of the size of the group, messaging is a closed system. Each user knows who sent the information and who received it. There are no hidden recipients.

SNS is a more open approach to communication. By comparison, it is a loudspeaker. All contacts view a user's information as it is posted. On Facebook, these announcements can be forwarded and shared over the entire internet, making content searchable by Google and other search engines. In addition, a user can go to a profile page and see everything that person has shared, including activities, other individuals, locations, voting practices, eating habits, and any other information that a user may share. A consequence of this is that incorrect or fraudulent information is shared as readily as legitimate posts. This has had dire consequences at several levels in recent years.

On the surface, Tencent and Facebook seem very similar. They are both platforms based around human social communication. If we need to use anchoring to understand Tencent, Facebook is the most straightforward Western equivalent. However, the comparative analogy quickly breaks down. Tencent and Facebook's monetization methods are different, their core strategies are different, and their product strategies are different. They are used differently. Facebook and Tencent live in two different worlds, as the Chinese internet world in which WeChat thrives is very different from the Western world in which Facebook dominates.

3

The Chinese Internet and WeChat

WeChat, or "WeiXin," means "micro message." However, it has become anything but micro. Today, WeChat is a behemoth with 1.2 billion monthly active users spending an annual US$15 trillion. (iResearch, 2021) Consider:

- Seventy-two million businesses accept WeChat Pay.
- Companies and organizations have more than 20 million official WeChat accounts and more than two million mini programs.
- WeChat's open platform has more than one million registered developers.

Businesses and developers involved with the WeChat app offer users a gold mine of value, fostering user activity and loyalty. The high concentration of active, loyal users spending money on the platform means that any business targeting the Chinese market must consider utilizing WeChat as an essential component of their marketing plan to be successful.

WeChat is still, first and foremost, a messaging platform, allowing people to message text and share pictures and different types of media with other individuals and groups. Secondly, WeChat, with the advent of the Moments feature, is a social media platform, or more specifically, an SNS. Thirdly, WeChat enables businesses to engage with people through Official Accounts (OA) and mini programs. An Official Account is akin to a business's homepage within WeChat, while mini programs are mini applications within the WeChat ecosystem. They are stars in WeChat's constellation of applications. Lastly, using incorporated payment, WeChat has become a financial tool and an ecommerce platform.

WeChat's ecosystem is comparable to a virtual city centered around a marketplace, a bustling place of activity, much like the bazaars of ancient times. Businesses are represented as peddlers in this metaphorical marketplace, selling their goods and services at market stalls. Developers are the builders, designing and constructing different storefronts for the peddlers to present their wares. Users are the visitors and buyers, venturing from their city homes to the marketplace to browse and acquire goods and services.

In this analogy, the WeChat application is both the marketplace and its environment. It provides the infrastructure that allows these parties to actively come together. It is also the surrounding city, a home for users to live and interact within. WeChat, as a company, is the governing body that oversees the marketplace and associated community. It provides not just the place but also the rules. WeChat guides how people interact. Strict developer and business regulations dictate how stalls are built and operated. New innovation is actively encouraged throughout all levels of the ecosystem.

Like any city, WeChat's impressive ecosystem wasn't built in a day. It was gradual and iterative and assembled on the foundations of China's unique environment at the time. To understand the intricacies of the WeChat story, its role in China's new digital revolution, then we must first go back to where it all began.

Splinternets

Most people believe and understand the world to have one internet, which is a constant, ubiquitous technology within which people and businesses connect. Yet, the internet can actually mean dramatically different things depending on the context and the people using it. For example, some people on the internet go to TikTok and watch videos, content, and photos. Other people learn on the platform. Others use the internet for gaming, having fun, entertainment, business, creativity, or research. Thus, the utility of the internet differs depending on the context and the user community.

The splinternet is a concept first proposed in 2001 to describe parallel internets that would run as distinct, private, and autonomous universes. (Crews, 2001) The term is applied when the internet is formally split into distinct components where content, services, and businesses only exist for those who have access to that particular piece. In this scenario, the internet is not a globe-spanning network of interconnected networks. Splinternets operate as discrete entities, often defined within geographic or demographic regions. On a massive nation scale, this is a relatively new phenomenon. However, the intranet concept has existed within a corporate environment, having their own company servers, even before the global internet. Intranets were explicitly designed to be used by a defined set of individuals in a closed setting. As such, they can also be defined as mini splinternets.

The splinternet is distinctly different from tailoring or customizing the internet. A network of networks can change to meet the preferences of an individual. For example, if I Google "shoes," Google knows who I am and has stored my data from my previous activities on the internet. My results, due to search engine optimization (SEO), will be designed just for me. Because

Google knows that I am male, Caucasian, 33-years old, and enjoy soccer and tennis, I'll probably see soccer shoes and tennis shoes. Since I have no sense of style, they will be comfortable walking shoes. And if I share my profile, it will be regionally based. What kind of shoe would someone like me, living in Australia, want to buy? The search results would differ from other regions where design trends, behavior, and climate might dictate different options. For example, you wouldn't offer fur-lined boots to someone living in a desert climate during summer.

Unlike the tailored internet where I order my shoes, the splinternet is widely available to a defined geographic or cultural group but is unavailable to those who are not part of that group. The global internet is one cohesive phenomenon. However, splinternets definitely exist for countries like Iran or North Korea, explicitly restricting what their citizens may access online. This is also true of China, but China has created something distinctly different. China's version of the splinternet was created to support a specific government, language, culture, and philosophy. Government influence provided the framework. The demographic characteristics that define the vast scope of China are the factors that allowed it to flourish, become so unique, and expand into a prolific, abundant, and rich ecosystem. It is an intranet in that it is a closed system, but unlike North Korea or Iran, it is not unidimensional.

Two features beyond geographic segregation distinguish splinternets and apply to China. The first is obstruction, where a government restricts content from coming into its territory. Internal censorship supports obstruction by preventing unwanted content from being created and disseminated within the country. The second factor is promotion, which is actively encouraging the growth of content that the government wants its citizens to see. These two factors are the push and pull of government influence over the internet. The most familiar of the two is obstruction – the infamous Great Firewall of China. However, subsidizing and supporting industry are also very important to understand how the internet and its contents developed in China.

These two aspects can be better understood with the metaphor of a walled garden. China's government has created a walled garden for the internet in China. The World Wide Web is analogous to flora that thrive anywhere and subsume native plants, which cannot compete with the more vigorous invaders. People in Australia easily understand this metaphor; native plant life and animal life can't compete with invasive or newly introduced species of flora and fauna. Australians protect their country from these invaders, enabling native wildlife to continue to flourish. Modern China tech, in its infancy, simply could not compete with global technologies that were developed amid intense competition in Europe or North America.

Similarly, China's government has created a walled garden that keeps things out through a combination of prohibition and deterrence symbolized by the wall. However, the wall encloses a thriving garden. China has cultivated native plants and is committed to ensuring that they flourish. It has nurtured its intranet, fostering content, business, and specific technologies, while creating new native technologies not seen outside the wall. China is not just trying to grow any technology within its walled garden or ecosystem. They are fostering their own internet with Chinese characteristics and new tech companies' native to China while ensuring that each has the space and nutrients to grow.

North Korea also has a walled garden to create its own internet ecosystem, keeping out foreign content and supporting its own internal content, but it lacks sufficient resources to support a vibrant ecosystem. It also lacks a self-sustaining consumer market, and economies of scale do not apply.

This could also be applied to countries like Iran, whose rulers have built their own walls, trying to cultivate their own content. They have a much larger scale than North Korea because their garden space includes a substantial portion of the Arab world. They also have a well-educated population, many of whom are graduates of US and European universities. Unlike North Korea, their isolation is relatively recent. However, it is a small country, the Iranian economy has suffered from international sanctions and been depleted by sectarian conflict. It doesn't have the resources or the market that China has. Like North Korea, Iran's internet-based economy has not thrived.

The walled garden metaphor is very apt for China. It enables tech companies to grow without competing with the greater outside world. If China had tried to grow the garden – its technology services – while competing with the vigorous "blackberry bushes" coming from Silicon Valley or "ivy" that strangles the competition, Tencent, Alibaba, and Baidu would never have existed or developed as they did. They needed that room to grow. Having grown, they needed the space to internally compete, evolve, and become more resilient.

Today, China's walled garden flourishes. In 2020, mobile payments in China were a whopping US$39 trillion, dwarfing the United States' US$197 billion by a factor of 180. (iResearch, 2021) Superapps are creating innovations and business models that didn't previously exist anywhere. And as the garden flourishes, it has begun to spill out over the walls. While the walls are definitely not coming down, the cultivated plants within are finding cracks and moving out into the global space:

- TikTok has become a global phenomenon
- Tencent is making forays into Southeast Asia and global

investments
- Alibaba's global business grows with extensive global investments
- DiDi is operating in dozens of countries

Hundreds more examples exist. One especially memorable example of China's unique tech spilling to overseas was stationless bike-share craze in 2017. Two companies, Mobike and Ofo Bike were, in fierce competition in China. As they moved to a global stage, appearing in cities worldwide at the corner of every street in every capital, they were competing within China for investors. Each wished to claim that it was the most successful Chinese-operated global bike-share company. As such, it deserved to be the all-out winner with investors. Like many platforms attempting to become international players, Ofo and Mobike didn't succeed because the business models were wrong for the world beyond the wall. Their model worked in China because it was designed for the Chinese market. Innovations like WeChat mini programs and ubiquitous digital payment made scanning and paying for bike shares easy. They developed their business in China, where 840 million people live in densely populated urban centers with highly effective public transportation systems and few cars. Ofo and Mobike were a welcome addition to the public transportation systems of China's cities. Still, they could not adapt to a population where they used mass transit and drove their own cars. Simply put, they were bred to thrive in the Chinese splinternet. While their business models worked well in China, they failed overseas.

Four factors cause a part of the internet to splinter off and become its own splinternet. The first three factors, language, culture, and scale are demographic and specific to the user community generating the demand for internet content. These factors define the consumer market.

- Language, spoken and written, significantly dictates the structure and content of the internet. Everything in China is obviously in Chinese and written in hanzi (Chinese characters). The Chinese language is spoken by the largest ethnic population in the world. The greater global internet uses primarily English. The sheer volume of Chinese speakers is sufficient justification for creating a China-specific internet.
- Chinese culture developed in geographic isolation, separated by the Himalayas and the plateaus of the central Asian steppes, which enabled a unique and complex culture and tradition.
- Scale refers to the size of China in all its aspects: geography, population, economy, diversity, and global influence. The demand for tools to support the unique language and culture of a massive population requires that it be scalable to accommodate current needs and future expansion.

The fourth factor is government, which generates the push and pull to allow the consumer market to split from the greater global market. The government keeps global content out, promoting certain content to grow within. The Chinese government created the circumstances for China to develop its own internet. Chinese scale provided the demand for how that internet grew. The government system, the political system, is a manifestation of Chinese culture and history. These factors worked together with the result that China's internet has quickly diverged from the rest of the world and prospered.

Many people, including then President of the US, Bill Clinton, didn't believe this was possible two decades ago. The internet was thought to be an uncontrollable democratic force of the user community. It was assumed that all nations would become interconnected through digital channels. Countries disconnected from the network would be left behind. But China would prove them wrong. These are the conditions under which Tencent and WeChat were created.

4

A Tale of Two Internets

Over a decade ago, I studied in Beijing at Peking University for a year. It was 2009, and smartphones had just hit the market. I didn't own one, but I did have a computer. Like the rest of the world, I enjoyed Googling the web. Unlike the rest of the world, I noticed that my Google search results in China were becoming conspicuously slower. Google had failed to comply with government content regulations. They were not self-censoring, and the government was ensuring that Google's performance suffered to ensure they understood that the Chinese government controlled the internet. Later that same year, Google pulled out of China. I walked the three blocks from my apartment in Haidian district to the headquarters of Google China. Local Google sympathizers had left flowers on the logo in a touching display of mourning.

Google's exit from China was unequivocally pivotal. China was developing its own unique internet with China-specific regulations, market opportunities, and trends. It was no longer an extension of the greater global internet. Google's exit created a void for Chinese tech companies to fill, further reinforcing China's unique digital ecosystem. As the world's internet evolved for different countries and cultures, internet diversity – the degree of difference among different geographic regions

– has increased. To better understand this process and how it contributed to China's unique digital ecosystem, let us examine basic definitions around the concept of the internet.

Merriam-Webster defines the internet as "an electronic communications network that connects computer networks and organizational computer facilities around the world." The internet is the hardware, the connected network of computer systems. The web, or World Wide Web, is the software which runs on that hardware. Colloquially the two terms are commonly used interchangeably. For simplicity, in this book I refer to the combined phenomenon of the hardware (internet) and software (web)as the 'internet'.

Yet, the internet to the common person is much more than a bunch of network servers and computer code. The internet is a tool that enables you to chat with friends, share photos, or read articles. It is a means to stay connected. It is searching for something on Google, posting a photo on Facebook, watching videos on YouTube, or bingeing TV shows on Netflix. The internet is something always at our fingertips, and each person's experience is intimate and unique.

However, these parameters are still infinitely broad. To strip back the concept of the internet to something more accessible, I suggest a more personal definition, the amalgamation of information and services accessible to an individual through a digital device. In other words, the things you can see or share with your smartphone or computer. This describes the internet through the lens of the user, which is how the common person views the internet.

As this definition is tied to the individual, and people's norms vary across the globe, the internet also varies from place to place. While Facebook, Google, YouTube, and Netflix may be popular in the West, this is not necessarily the case in other parts of the world. An individual in China searches via Baidu; in India, she shops online with Flipkart; and in Brazil, she orders a taxi with Grab; and in the US she uses Craigslist to shop for second-hand goods. I use the term 'internet diversity' to describe how the internet a person experiences changes based on factors, such as geographic region and government.

When the internet was conceived, it was fairly uniform. Initially developed in the United States and United Kingdom (with participation from organizations in France), all coding languages were in English, and Western countries generated most of the content.

As more countries contributed to and used the internet, its diversity increased. While virtually all coding languages are still based in English, the content on the internet is now in thousands of different languages catering to people worldwide. In addition, varying policies, companies, pop culture trends, events, and more have added to the diversity of the internet.

Commonly, nations with unique needs have minimal impact on global internet trends. For example, the Fijian Pidgin English bible app, "Tok Pisin Baibel," fills a small niche. Its target market, the population of Fiji, is just shy of one million people. The market demand might feed a few independent developers but is too small to sustain a major tech company. Therefore, small content such as this bible app will be the only Fiji-specific digital content developers will create. By contrast, China's massive 1.4 billion population makes unique solutions economically viable, leading to a world of possibilities and a separate and distinct internet.

I have narrowed down the influences on internet diversity to the four factors previously described, i.e., language, culture, government, and scale. In broad terms, a nation's language and culture largely determine whether it adopts existing internet content and design or innovates its own solutions. Government policies and infrastructure further influence a country's approach. Finally, as evidenced by Fiji vs. China, scale determines whether these solutions have global economic significance. In the coming chapters, these influences are discussed in greater detail.

5

Language

Language is the first contributing factor to internet diversity. In the digital age, English has become the lingua franca or common tongue. More than half of the world's digital content is in English. Since its inception, English-speaking American firms, especially those in Silicon Valley, have dominated digital applications and the internet. Virtually all coding languages are in English.

The predominance of English creates a barrier for the non-English speaking world, which encourages internet diversity. Although website developers typically use multilingual development platforms, such as Wix, Weebly, or WordPress, tools other than English are difficult to find. A Japanese speaker building a website will struggle to find a coding language or developer help articles in Japanese characters. However, from this challenge comes the opportunity to engineer Japanese-specific solutions that do not conform to the English-centric internet norm.

The size and concentration of the population and the degree of deviation from English influence internet diversity. Most Chinese speakers live in China. While there are many local languages and dialects - 302 living languages according to one estimate - most people speak some version of the north Chinese language, of which Mandarin is a dialect. Nearly everyone in the country for whom Mandarin is not a primary language speaks

Mandarin as a second language. Also, all Chinese languages use a standardized written system of Chinese characters. As China has a literacy rate of 96.4%, approximately 1.35 billion of China's 1.4 billion population read and write in Chinese characters.

The Chinese language has a significant scale within China, but it doesn't stop there. Globally, the number of native Chinese speakers, those for whom Chinese is their first language, is on par with the total number of English speakers worldwide, native and non-native, at approximately 1.5 billion. The number of native English speakers is approximately 360 million individuals, about 24% of the total number of native Chinese speakers.

Mandarin Chinese is vastly different from English. This difference is easily gauged by how difficult it is for an English speaker to learn Mandarin Chinese. The United States Foreign Service (USFS) classifies Chinese in an exclusive group of Super-hard languages, which are exceptionally difficult for native English speakers to learn. There are only three other languages in this group, Arabic, Japanese, and Korean. In certain situations, factors beyond language differences could contribute to the ease or difficulty of language acquisition; however, the professionalism of the USFS makes their ranking parameters credible. For example, a potential lack of educational material is overcome by the USFS's resources. Higher demand for aptitude in particular languages is managed by the USFS's standardized target on the Interagency Language Roundtable scale. The more languages diverge, the greater the language barrier. As most of the internet is created with and operates in English, the Chinese language faces one of the most significant entry barriers worldwide.

Just as differences widen a language barrier, similarities reduce it. A common language decreases communication barriers and can also promote similar legal and business systems. For example, while Austria and Germany are two different countries, both share a Germanic past and utilize the German language, which has resulted in similar legal and financial systems. I saw this firsthand during WeChat Pay's global expansion when payment partners in Germany could also easily engage the Austrian market and vice-versa.

This is not always the case, though, and countries that share a language may possess vastly different financial and legal systems. As a result, many websites, such as Apple, Airbnb, Uber, and many more, initially request that users specify their country so that the website content is optimized for the correct nationality.

Aside from the financial and legal practicalities of triaging users based on nationality, this also allows companies to target users more effectively by using country-specific vernacular, slang, or "dialects." For example, English websites often differ among British English, Australian English, and US English by including local language preferences to make the websites more relatable to users.

Whether specifying a language for marketing and communication or more pragmatic purposes, such as currency, legal, or shipping processes, language retains a significant influence on the diversity of the internet. In addition, language elements like slang and linguistic preferences cross the line into "cultural influence," which is equally important in defining internet diversity.

Figure 2: eBay's Greetings.

eBay tweaks its content to resonant more with different English-speaking countries

6

CULTURE: HISTORY, CELEBRATION, AND BELIEF

THE SECOND FACTOR influencing internet diversity is culture. Culture encompasses many parameters, such as history, national celebration, ideology, religion, social structure, and how culture has evolved and adapted. Given our user-centric definition of the internet and the observation that user behavior is influenced by culture, the very existence of cultural diversity predicts internet diversity. With this comes a variety of user solutions to suit cultural preferences, of which WeChat is one such solution.

China's History of Isolation

China has enjoyed a rich history - approximately 5,000 years - of isolation. Geographic isolation, with oceans in the east, the Himalayas in the west, and warring tribes to the north, led China to evolve independently from the rest of the world. This segregated history created a complex and totally unique culture.

The Cultural Dimensions Framework was developed by the Dutch psychologist Geert Hofstede. It is a valuable and objective tool that has been used to describe how Chinese culture diverges from that of other parts of the world. Hofstede defines culture as "the collective programming of the mind distinguishing the members of one group or category of people from others." His framework delineates national cultural traits into six dimensions:

- Power Distance Index, which looks at the distribution of power within a society. A high score means that a society accepts a hierarchical order.
- Individualism vs. Collectivism refers to the degree of societal cohesion.
- Masculinity vs. Femininity, in simple terms, is the difference between tough vs. tender behavior.
- Uncertainty Avoidance is the degree to which a culture or group is comfortable with uncertainty and ambiguity.
- Long-Term Orientation vs. Short-Term Normative Orientation references how readily a society encourages and adapts to change.
- Indulgence vs. Restraint is a continuum of indulgence or the acceptance of behavior to restrained or suppressed society with strict social norms.

According to Hofstede's research, China's society stands out in three dimensions: Power Distance, Individualism, and Long-Term Orientation. China's high Power Distance score reflects a strong belief in hierarchies while acknowledging and accepting that power should be distributed unequally. This tends to produce an acquiescent society that respects and responds to authority with minimal divisiveness. The Individualism score suggests that China's culture is collectivist (a term associated with socialist or communist societies) and often acts in the group's interest as opposed to the individual. Finally, the Long-Term Orientation score demonstrates China's tendency to adapt or modify tradition to meet changing conditions. Chinese are likely to save, invest, and persevere for future goals rather than self-gratify; this distinction is also referred to as a Normative vs. Pragmatic approach. (Hofstede Insights, 2022)

These traits, burned into the Chinese culture over thousands of years in isolation, play a crucial role in determining personal identity and behavior. Understanding this historical evolution and its impact is vital to understanding Chinese people today.

With history comes the commemoration of national holidays. Today's China celebrates Chinese holidays that represent significant markers of cultural celebration and encourage particular traditions and customs. China, unlike the West, traditionally follows the Lunar calendar, not the Gregorian calendar (a solar calendar). The most essential calendar holiday is the Chinese New Year or the Spring Festival. This week-long holiday occurs at the beginning of the new year on the Lunar calendar. The other week-long holiday is National Day, which commemorates the establishment of the People's Republic of China (PRC) on October 1st. Besides these, there are five single-day holidays: Tomb-Sweeping Day, Labor Day, Dragon Boat Festival, Mid-Autumn Festival, and the (International) New Year.

Of the eleven days of public holidays, only two align with the West: Labor Day on May 1st and (International) New Year's Day on January 1st. The rest are China-specific. The widespread celebration of culturally unique holidays tends to reinforce a sense of shared cultural identity. Cultural identity is also reinforced by adhering to traditions or practicing common societal beliefs. For example, the color red, the number eight, and the gifting of red packets are all significant in China. These unique traditions and holidays illustrate the diversion of China from Western norms. They are another set of features that has encouraged the splinternet.

While many national holidays around the world are a component of religious practice, and particular religions have played a significant part in the evolution of culture, religion plays a very minor role in China. The traditional monotheistic concept of religion as a belief system centered around a divine creator is historically absent in China. Officially, China's government supports atheism. The majority of the population practice Chinese folk religions and rituals and celebrate festivals to varying degrees without ascribing to institutionalized teaching or belief. Philosophical teachings from Confucianism, Taoism, and Buddhism, often called the "three teachings," are engrained in the wider Chinese consciousness. These represent a broader concept of religion. They offer a set of life principles and a practice intended to model behavior. Their focus is on day-to-day activities rather than working toward an afterlife.

This differs from much of the rest of the world and the West. The overwhelming majority follow monotheistic religions such as Christianity, Islam, and Judaism, or polytheistic religions like Hinduism. Some Western governments incorporate religion into their governing philosophy, as in the US, "In God we trust," written on the currency, or the phrase, "all men are created equal under God." These religions establish different moral codes and belief systems from those dictated by China's atheism or local folk traditions, further contributing to the cultural distance between China and the West.

China's belief systems, including Chinese folk religions and the "three teachings," though not religious in the traditional theistic sense, comprise key attributes of the Chinese ethos. Much like national holidays, these belief systems feed directly into the Chinese cultural identity. Entwined with history, these elements have contributed to the development of a unique Chinese culture. This has produced Chinese digital technology consumers for whom the traditional World Wide Web is insufficient. Again, the result is the desire for an internet divergent from the Western norm.

7

GOVERNMENT

WHILE THERE is overlap with history, government systems play a direct role in influencing internet diversity. Considering that internet diversity reflects user experience, the government's influence can be measured by how much pressure it exerts over its user community. Two confluent forces determine the Chinese government's impact: its ability to control or protect and the people's desire to be controlled or protected by the government. Note that the words "control" and "protect" are semantically subjective. Meaning is determined by whether the influence is perceived as negative or positive.

China's political history and the Communist Party of China (CPC) subsequent approach to the internet highlight a key point: the government's ability and the population's desire to close off China from the outside world have existed to some degree for millennia. Today, this protectionist attitude contributes directly to China's digital segregation and internet diversity globally.

Following centuries of outside interference in China, modern China's governing body inherited a mandate to protect the population from the outside world. Prior to attempts at colonization from both Western and Eastern nations, China's isolation fostered independence and self-reliance that produced a great civilization and a leading force in technology and trade.

China is credited with making some of the most significant technical contributions of the pre-industrial era, including paper-making, the compass, gunpowder manufacturing, and the printing press. These developments bolstered their efforts in exploration, warfare, and institutionalized education. Advancements like these strengthened China's economy and international trade. The Silk Road (or Silk Routes) was established more than 2,000 years ago as a series of multinational trade thoroughfares that enabled China to access and provide goods to the global market. In the West, we say, "all roads lead to Rome." It might be more historically accurate to say, "all roads lead to Xi'an," which was the center of Chinese silk production, the capital of the Han dynasty and the true starting point of the Silk Road.

China was a global power for centuries and had developed a trade-based economy. However, it was sufficiently robust and comfortable with isolation to defend and protect its boundaries. In the 15th Century, after a string of naval explorations by Admiral Zheng He, the Ming Dynasty closed the country to foreign trade. This was done with relatively little backlash from the outside world. However, this all changed during the Qing Dynasty when the ruling Manchus refused to open up to foreign trade under pressure from Britain and other Western countries. As Western powers, later joined by Japan, pushed for trading rights, the Opium War took place in 1839-1842, followed by the Boxer Rebellion in 1900. Ultimately, foreign powers triumphed and forcibly established large-scale trading operations in Hong Kong, Shanghai, and other ports along the China coast. During this time, the Qing empire lost a significant degree of autonomy over its economy, leading to a major weakening of its sovereignty. Ultimately, China ceded property to Japan, Russia, and various European countries. By the early 1900s, dynastic China was weak and forced to surrender additional land to its aggressive neighbor, Japan, sparking China's transition from a kingdom to a republic in 1911. Japan's thirst for land led to the invasion of Manchuria, which Japan occupied until its surrender in 1945.

This historical tension between openness and isolationism generated long-standing Chinese caution about relegating any aspect of control. Particularly following the Japanese occupation, the Chinese population was yearning for a new, more muscular political system that could withstand, among other things, foreign control and invasion. The answer, in the end, was the Communist Revolution.

In this context, in its ascent to power following the civil war of the late 1940s, the CPC has continued to exercise caution about opening China to the rest of the world. This has been apparent across the board in trade, immigration, education, and the relatively modern internet frontier.

The CPC's Approach to the Internet

The CPC embraced the internet while implementing measures of control that would ultimately divert the Chinese user experience from that of the rest of the world. This began when the internet first came into existence in the 1980s when Communist China began re-opening its borders following the Cultural Revolution. Then, as the World Wide Web started to boom in the mid-1990s, the CPC, recognizing the range of opportunities that broad access to the internet offered, also understood that the internet opened China as profoundly as the shipping channels of the previous century. As a result, the CPC understood that maintaining control meant curating the internet, which they have done for the last 40 years.

When the internet was a new digital frontier, many experts questioned whether government influence of the sort the CPC intended was possible. Internet Idealists, including Vinton Cerf, also known as 'The Father of the Internet,' believed that the internet was an uncontrollable phenomenon "... designed without any contemplation of national boundaries." (Goldmish & Wu, 2008) Cerf and others predicted that the internet would degrade the importance of the nation-state. They believed that it would organize the world into online social structures with freedom of information, speech, and assembly regardless of geopolitical location. Conversely, Internet Realists believed that as the internet was a tool invented by humans, it could also be manipulated by humans. They predicted that the internet could be used and controlled by existing political, economic, and social structures, effectively transferring geographic borders into the virtual universe.

Some countries, including Bahrain, the United Arab Emirates, Saudi Arabia, and Iran, demonstrated that digital boundaries were largely enforceable. These governments exercised internet filtering on political, social, and security content. Case-specific filtering and restrictions also began to emerge, which posed new challenges to nation-state law. Yet, an early example of enforcing geographic borders on the internet was not found in one of these nations, but in Western Europe. In the year 2000, a lawsuit was levied against Yahoo for violating a French law that banned the sale and purchase of Nazi-related goods in France. Yahoo.fr complied, but French users could still access the US website, effectively bypassing the French law. To fully comply, Yahoo would have to apply the requirements of the French law to all its servers, affecting its users globally. Infosplit, an internet company, provided a method of identifying and screening internet content based on a user's geographical location. Effectively, contrary to early prediction, the internet gained and enforced geographic boundaries to conform to national law.

During these early days, China sought to enforce geographic and political boundaries through its "Golden Shield Project," which it established in 1998. This was a government apparatus that blocked online content and services deemed illegal under Chinese law. Internationally, the project is infamous for systematically blocking and slowing access to certain foreign websites and content. This process later became known as "The Great Firewall of China." Other nations saw these control efforts as futile, echoing the sentiments of the Internet Idealists. During President Bill Clinton's 1998 visit to China, he remarked, "There's no question China has been trying to crack down on the internet—good luck. (laughter). That's sort of like trying to nail Jell-O to the wall. (laughter)." (Goldmish & Wu, 2008)

Fast forward to 2022, and China-specific internet laws are no joke. Domestic and foreign companies operating legally in China have to comply with Chinese law, including the blocking and deletion of content considered to be illicit and providing the government with information on specific users. While the Chinese government was not the first to control the internet within their geographic borders, the "Golden Shield Project" has become the most potent internet controlling apparatus in the world. As a result, global tech companies, which have traditionally functioned under Internet Idealist beliefs, have difficulty operating within China's terms. For example, Google faced a backlash from their home countries when complying with "Golden Shield Project" guidelines, which resulted in Google effectively exiting China in 2010. Today, this is a significant barrier to entry for foreign companies wishing to expand into the Chinese market.

However, the inability of international companies to adjust to the Chinese legal requirements provides an opportunity for Chinese companies to fill the gaps, which the Chinese government actively supports. In its 13th economic five-year plan, released on March 17th, 2016, the CPC's primary focus was utilizing innovative technology to improve peoples' lives. Tech companies were encouraged to provide solutions for government and financial services. "Internet+," which Tencent's CEO Pony Ma lobbied to see, would lead to the development of digital solutions within different industrial verticals. Government collaboration and top-down support saw popular mobile apps like WeChat and Alipay incorporate functions that could pay gas, water, electricity bills, traffic fines, and parking fees. These functions evolved to more complex services, such as applying for entry permits to Hong Kong and Macau, registering marriages, and all non-face-to-face services at Public Hospitals, which treat most patients in China. As well as bolstering digital services, the CPC also supported domestic mobile payment solutions and ecommerce platforms, leading to an unprecedented rise in digital transactions.

As governments shape their national laws and censorship parameters, the subsequent regional separation increases internet diversity. How important these factors are to the global community is primarily determined by the scale of their impact.

8

Scale

The fourth factor influencing internet diversity is scale. Unlike the previous three factors, scale cannot generate diversity. Rather, it determines how significant a country's digital difference is in relation to the rest of the world. Scale, in this context, is not just determined by population size but also by purchasing power. In particular, as it pertains to this discussion, China's massive scale and the individual purchasing power of each Chinese smartphone user are significant in understanding and predicting the impact of scale. Without scale, China's unique internet, and, subsequently, WeChat, would not have the global significance and impact they do.

In China, the three previous factors have created a sufficiently diverse internet that functions as an incubator for fledgling Chinese tech companies by restricting access to or the incursion of the outside internet. However, if these factors are the primary delimiter, scale is the factor that contributes to endless growth from within. By focusing solely on the domestic market, scale enables Chinese companies to expand within a predictable and well-understood environment with equivalent competition restricted to other Chinese companies. In addition, by remaining local, Chinese companies turn Chinese language, culture, and government, which are major barriers for outsiders, into strategic advantages.

China's digital market is a behemoth, with nearly a billion smartphone users. That's more than the trailing three largest smartphone market countries combined (India has 493 million, US has 274 million, and Indonesia has 170 million). Unfortunately, not all smartphone users are created equal. User purchasing power generates demand, which attracts digital business. A nation's population composed of sufficiently wealthy smartphone users will provide significant opportunities for companies to develop solutions within the internet environment. This is the case for China, but how do you calculate the purchasing power of smartphone users for further comparison?

Currently, there is no market standard measurement for this purpose. To overcome this, I have developed an index by multiplying a country's GDP by the percentage of its population that uses smartphones. I call this the Gross Smartphone User Market (GSUM). GSUM estimates the overall market power created by smartphone users of any particular country. China's GSUM is its GDP of US$16.6 trillion, multiplied by its smartphone penetration of 66%, which equals US$10.98 trillion.

The GSUM calculation provides enlightening comparisons. After China, the next largest smartphone market is India. India has a total GDP of $3 trillion, with a 35% smartphone penetration rate, giving India a GSUM of around US$1 trillion. While China's smartphone users are roughly double India's, China's GSUM is ten times greater than India's. This means that China's smartphone users generate roughly ten times the domestic market power and consequent demand for digital services. Applying the GSUM calculation to more countries yields further insights.

As seen in Figure 3, China's GSUM is a robust second behind the United States. The next runner-up, Japan, has a GSUM nearly three times smaller than China's. The United States and China have the scale necessary to incubate large-scale digital businesses within their local markets. However, the presence of the other three factors of internet diversity set these two countries apart. American companies have far lower cultural, linguistic, and governmental barriers to global expansion. They have the luxury at most stages in their growth cycle of selling to their large-scale local market or expanding internationally. This contributes heavily to the global ubiquity of American tech companies.

	Country	Smartphone Users (mil)	Population (mil)	Smartphone Penetration	GDP* (bil)	GSUM (bil)
1	United States	274	333	82%	22,675	18,639
2	China	954	1,440	66%	16,642	10,984
3	Germany	83	126	66%	5,378	3,544
4	Japan	66	84	79%	4,319	3,403
5	United Kingdom	54	68	80%	3,125	2,494
6	France	52	65	79%	2,938	2,315
7	Italy	47	60	77%	2,106	1,622
8	Russia	102	146	70%	1,711	1,199
9	India	493	1,390	35%	3,049	1,079
10	Brazil	119	214	55%	1,491	826
11	Indonesia	170	276	62%	1,159	715
12	Mexico	75	130	57%	1,192	684
13	Turkey	55	85	65%	795	515
14	Iran	57	85	67%	683	460
15	Thailand	41	70	59%	539	320
16	Vietnam	67	98	68%	355	242
17	Philippines	46	111	41%	403	166
18	Bangladesh	61	166	37%	353	130
19	Nigeria	42	211	20%	514	101
20	Pakistan	47	225	21%	286	60

Figure 3: Top 20 Gross Smartphone User Markets (GSUM).

*The GSUM provides a rough estimate of purchase power of smartphone users, and therein, demand for digital content for a country. *Note: Measured in Nominal GDP for its ubiquity and relevance in global tech comparisons. (Newzoo, 2021; IMF, 2021)*

In contrast, Chinese tech companies tend to stay at home. The factors that hinder a foreign business from entering China also hinder Chinese business from expanding globally. Fortunately, China's scale is sufficiently large that its tech businesses prosper by focusing solely on the domestic market.

This monumental scale also entices international businesses to brave the challenges of an entirely new internet. The more a country differs from China in its language, culture, and government, the more difficult it is to conform to this new context. Japanese or Korean companies find it easier than European or American. Selling to the Chinese market now means international companies must pivot their strategies to work within the Chinese internet framework, understanding and utilizing local tools like WeChat.

9

Internet Diversity in the Real World

Examining the four factors that create internet diversity shows that the internet is complex and multifaceted. A homogenous global network no longer exists. China's internet, inclusive of its unique domestic companies, is the ultimate example of this. Before plunging into the intricacies of one product within this space, examples of competitive internet diversity in practice will add contextual depth to the discussion. This section unpacks two examples from geographic and industry-specific perspectives.

Geographic - West and East

As previously stated, all four factors influence a country's internet diversity and subsequent global importance. The United Kingdom has significant scale with a large GSUM of US$2.5 trillion. However, because its language is English, it aligns with the default language of the greater internet. The government does not create significant barriers or provide assistance to digital business development, so its internet is not particularly unique. France has some internet diversity because the French language encompasses 274 million speakers worldwide. However, the French language is relatively similar to English as determined by the USFS. Their respective cultures are also similar.

The internet of Asian countries, on the other hand, is

significantly diverse. Again, though, without scale this doesn't result in any major tech companies, and therefore doesn't manifest a major splintering from the greater internet. Vietnam is a good example. The Vietnamese language is substantially different from English, as it is classified as a Category III language by the USFS. Vietnam's distinctive culture is the result of thousands of years with little Western interaction or influence. Vietnam's government curates internet content using its 'bamboo firewall.' It is labeled an "Enemy of the Internet" by Reporters without Borders.

Based on the first three factors, Vietnam is similar to China. So, what is missing? Clearly, the answer is scale. Vietnam's scale is nowhere near China's, making its internet diversity relatively insignificant in the global context. Vietnam has a GDP of US$355 billion and a smartphone penetration rate of 68%, giving it a GSUM of US$242 billion. This is nearly 50 times smaller than China's GSUM. Unsurprisingly, Vietnam does not have many tech companies relevant to the global internet to withstand international competition.

While this is the case for Vietnam as an individual country, the consolidated nations of the Association of Southeast Asian Nations (ASEAN) lead to a different conclusion. ASEAN's ten core member countries (Indonesia, Malaysia, the Philippines, Singapore, Thailand, Brunei, Vietnam, Laos, Myanmar, and Cambodia) have a combined GSUM of US$2.2 trillion. The cultures, languages, and government systems of the ASEAN region are sufficiently unified to create significant internet diversity. While individually these countries alone lack scale, combined, their scale is substantial. This ensures that the ASEAN region can provide local digital services for itself.

Industry Case – Ride-hailing Apps

One industry that illustrates the power of scalable internet diversity is the ride-hailing industry during global proliferation and Uber's expansion in 2015. Across the world, various ride-hailing apps battled their dominance in different countries and regions. This battle perfectly portrayed the impact of the four factors that bring about internet diversity. The stronger the combined barriers to the greater Internet, the larger the ride-hailing apps the region was able to produce.

The Western champion, Uber, was the global standard – the equivalent of the Anglo-centric internet. The higher a region's barrier to entry, as dictated by the four factors, the larger the opportunity for a local company to emerge and grow. Therefore, a region's ride-share company value was directly proportional to its language, culture, government, and scale factors. In 2015, China's Didi and Yidao were worth a combined US$18 billion, India's OlaCabs US$2.5 billion, ASEAN's GrabTaxi US$1.5 billion. The market value of the competitors demonstrated the impact of the four factors on the regions ability to create barriers to Uber and give local players room to grow and prosper. (Chen & Huet, 2015)

Notice that Vietnam alone did not produce a strong competitor to Uber, instead the ASEAN region as a whole gave rise to GrabTaxi, which was a force to be reckoned with. In the end, Uber merged with GrabTaxi before exiting the country. India also retained its home-grown Ola ride-share app. However, Uber's greatest battle globally was with Didi (or "Didi Chuxing") in China. Uber reportedly spent US$2 billion in rider and driver incentives. Still, in the end, the local Didi outperformed the global Uber. In late 2016, Uber followed its strategy in Vietnam and merged with Didi, pulling out of China. Uber sold their China operations to Didi in exchange for a 20% stake in Didi and an investment from Didi of US$1 billion in Uber at a US$68 billion valuation. While both Uber and Didi left the negotiating table happy, Didi won the battle for the Chinese market. The New York Times wrote that with this deal, "[Uber would] join the ranks of American peers like Google and eBay, which were unable to capitalize on early footholds in China. eBay was outmaneuvered by Alibaba, while Google left China after it said it was the target of government-sponsored cyberattacks." (Mozur & Isaac, 2016)

China's homegrown competitors and the high barrier to foreign entry are not exclusive to the ride-share industry. This is one of the many obstacles that foreign companies face when trying to enter the China market. So, why bother? The answer is clearly that the monumental scale of China makes the value of success worth the risk. The Chinese market currently represents a large section of the global economy, with many industries and companies looking for opportunities for penetration. Smartphone utilization in China is high, and each person spends an average of more than 77 minutes a day on WeChat. This single mobile phone application represents a holy grail to unlock the secrets of the Chinese consumer.

Part 2

The WeChat Story

Part 2 tells the detailed story of WeChat from a project within Tencent to becoming the first 'Superapp' and one of the most valuable products in the world. This story starts with a preface of Tencent which was the company to incubate WeChat. Next is the proper WeChat story broken into four parts which were the four phases of WeChat's coming-of-age story; viral growth, connecting businesses, payments, and lastly, creating an efficient ecosystem.

10

CREATION

WECHAT'S story is guided by innovation focused on user value and effective responses to emerging market forces. Understanding WeChat's history and pivotal moments provides the groundwork to understand WeChat's secrets of success. This is the step-by-step story, simplified into major segments, of how Tencent started as a copy-cat company, and then went on to create the world's first Superapp.

Tencent

WeChat's story begins with the creation of its parent company, Tencent. Its founder and current CEO, Pony Ma (Ma Huateng), cultivated a culture of commitment to user value, product excellence, and competitive internal innovation. These were the necessary ingredients for Tencent to hire and empower entrepreneur Allen Zhang. He would go on to create Tencent's most popular product, WeChat.

Pony Ma was born in the southeast of China in Shantou, Guangdong province, in 1971. His family was of the Chaoshan culture, people from the Chaozhou and Shantou region known for their unique dialect, excellent cuisine, and for producing successful businesspeople, such as Li Ka-shing, the wealthiest person in Hong Kong and 42nd in the world according to

Forbes in 2021. During my four years at Tencent, I observed that the company employed many Chaoshan people, easily the company's largest ethnic grouping. They rallied behind their rising star, Pony Ma. In internal meetings, disagreements would commonly digress into an eruption of chatter in the Chaoshan dialect. With their distinct culture and language, Chaoshan (also called Chiuchow, Teochew or Teo-swa) people are insular. They enjoy doing business and keeping their affairs within the family, or amongst greater Chaoshan people, as they did at Tencent.

Pony's family moved from Shantou to the island of Hainan when his father gained employment at the local port authority. Thanks to Hainan's clean air and low light pollution, Pony grew up under a brilliant night sky full of stars – a luxury now missing in most Chinese cities. This experience helped to inspire an early interest in the heavens. While his parents were not particularly wealthy, Pony eventually convinced them to buy him a telescope, one of his childhood's most prized possessions. Later in life, Pony would reflect that winning a small cash prize for photographing Halley's Comet in 1986 was the proudest moment of his life. (Hu, 2017)

In 1984, Pony's father acquired a new job at Shenzhen's Port Authority and moved his family to Shenzhen. Pony enrolled in Shenzhen University in 1989. At a time when Shenzhen's technical prowess was growing, and with the pragmatism typical of Chaoshan people, Pony chose to forgo a degree in Astronomy to pursue his education in Computer Science.

Pony transferred his passion for the stars to the realm of information technology by building a company at the forefront of Chinese innovation. By creating Tencent, Pony launched an entire digital universe, or "QQ-verse," for Chinese people to enjoy. Decades later, around 2017, Pony directed investments into three different projects in the outer space industry. While many investors believed this foreshadowed a strategic shift for Tencent, those closer to Pony knew this was more a man indulging his childhood dreams.

After graduating from university in 1993, Pony joined a company called Runxun Communications. At Runxun, he earned just $176 a month developing software for pagers. Five years later, Pony left the job to start a company. In 1998, Pony Ma founded Tencent with four classmates: Chen Yidan Chen, Xu Chenye, Zeng Liqing, and Zhang Zhidong. The name, Tencent (or 腾讯) comes from a combination of the second character of Pony's name, Teng (or 腾) and the second character of the Runxun, Xun (or 讯), which was then translated to "cent." Tencent's first office space was a few small rooms in a central office building in the Futian district of Shenzhen. While the team quickly outgrew this first office, it is preserved today as a corporate museum and used for internal training videos, such as educating new employees on company culture and celebrating Tencent's anniversary.

Initially, the Tencent team's goal was to develop telecommunications software. However, this goal pivoted after Pony saw a presentation on ICQ, an Israeli instant messaging program released in 1996. ICQ had already become the world's first globally popular instant messaging program. However, there was no Chinese version, which presented Pony with a unique opportunity.

In 1999, Pony and his team developed and launched OICQ or "Open ICQ," essentially a Chinese-language and China-localized version of ICQ. OICQ reached 1 million registered users in nine months, quickly becoming one of the largest messaging programs in China.

Tencent's long-term strategy is best classified as "hybrid innovation" rather than pure imitation despite the apparent outside influence. Their products combined old or existing technology with new localized elements, rapidly evolving as something unique. Pony believed that "to copy is not evil." From the beginning, it was no secret that external inspiration was a core Tencent strategy in developing new products.

Copyright Woes

However, not everyone saw Tencent's copy strategy as harmless. In March 2000, AOL (America Online), which had acquired ICQ two years earlier, took legal action against Tencent, claiming that "OICQ" violated ICQ's copyright. AOL won the lawsuit, and Tencent changed OICQ's name to QQ. QQ was a strategic play on words, with the letter "Q" signifying "cute" in Chinese popular culture. The idea was that "QQ" would be "double cute" and enter the hearts and homes of Chinese twice as fast.

To avoid further legal action, Tencent also removed other copyrighted content from the QQ platform. This included

Figure 4: OICQ's avatars in 1999.

Can you spot the copyrighted material? (Sohu, 2022)

removing avatars (see Figure 4) which were obviously characters from the Simpsons, Pokémon, the Flintstones, Popeye, Tom and Jerry, the Smurfs, and other popular franchises.[1] Tencent then centered its brand image around the now-iconic penguin, selected for the same simple reason as QQ; penguins were cute and friendly. Reflecting on this period in a rare interview years later, Pony paraphrased Isaac Newton's famous phrase. "When we were a small company, we needed to stand on the shoulders of giants to grow up." (Wang, Xing, 2009)

Early Days

Despite their swift user adoption, Tencent struggled to transition to product monetization. As users and user activity rose, so did maintenance and server costs. The company's handful of small revenue streams were insufficient to support the product. "We knew our product had a future, but at that time, we just couldn't afford it." The young company was broke.

However, remember Chaoshan people generally like to keep things within the family and the Chaoshan network. Pony was no exception. In Tencent's early days, Pony's mother was the company's legal representative, and his father was the accountant. When the company needed capital, the Chaoshan network provided a connection to the son of the aforementioned Chaoshan billionaire, Li Ka-shing, who ran Pacific Century Cyberworks (PCCW), an important telecom carrier. This introduction produced a 20 percent investment in Tencent, valued at US$5.5 million in the year 2000. In addition, an American investment firm, IDC, joined the capital-raising round,

1 In 2019, Tencent's ISUX (Interactive Social User Experience) team posted a nostalgic redesign of old QQ avatars. While they obviously attempted to exclude copyright material, somehow Brutus, the villain from Popeye, was overlooked. Go to this url to see how Brutus sticks out like a sore thumb in the modern redesign for an interesting laugh: https://isux.tencent.com/articles/qq-retro-avatar

also investing a 20 percent stake. Now with US$2.2 million in financial capital, Tencent had time to continue to expand its user base and test various monetization techniques.

Later that same year, Tencent established a successful method of monetization that would account for 80% of Tencent's revenue. First, the company enabled its QQ desktop client to send text (SMS) messages directly to mobile phones. Then, utilizing relationships and Pony's background with telecom carriers, Tencent struck deals that landed a share of the SMS fee revenue. Tencent would go on to attempt and test varied monetization strategies. Predictably, they sold advertising on the QQ ecosystem. Less conventionally, they integrated various products and user services and offered purchasing functionality. Tencent called these "value-added services." They ranged from customizable avatars to web-based games with in-game purchases and more. In 2002, Tencent even released a digital currency, "QQ coin," to make transactions easier within their online ecosystem. This was one of the earliest forms of a digital currency, predating Bitcoin by half a decade, and had surprisingly high adoption and circulation. (Wang & Mainwaring, April)

Fast forward to the beginning of 2005, and Tencent's ecosystem was flourishing. Tencent launched:

- QQ games, which became China's most popular casual game portal
- QQ.com, a news portal, which as of September 2021, was the fourth most popular website in the world according to the web traffic-analysis platform Alexa Internet
- RTX (Real-Time eXchange), an instant messaging product optimized for businesses.

Tencent's value-added services extended the product

offerings with QQ messenger, the social glue that held the ecosystem together.

Despite these successes, by 2005, Tencent was losing the battle in one crucial field: email. Two years after its launch, QQmail lagged behind the competition. With fewer than 1 million users, Tencent's email service was not even among China's top ten email providers. This could potentially have subverted Tencent's entire ecosystem. Email was strategically important to Tencent, as it was a frequent use-case generating user traffic, and also it provided a user's online identity. An email identifier was used to register for various programs all over the internet. If another company's email service began diverting users, Tencent would lose a significant portion of its social monopoly.

Fortunately, Tencent had money. In 2004, the company publicly listed on the Hong Kong Stock Exchange with a market value of US$1 billion. (Gopalan, 2004) This gave Tencent the required capital to maintain and grow its services, as well as the prospect of mergers and acquisitions. One major acquisition in March 2005, was Foxmail, one of the most popular email services. More importantly, Foxmail was founded by one of China's rising tech stars, Allen Zhang.

Allen and Pony had a great deal in common. They were developers-turned-entrepreneurs who became managers. Both had an incredibly user-centric view of doing business, which came from developing products to create user value. When it came to developing products, both were proud perfectionists. Pony once said that he had tested every piece of instant messaging software Tencent had ever released. At WeChat, Allen similarly tested and approved every minute change to the product.

Their personalities were similar in even more aspects than their professionalism. Unlike Alibaba founder Jack Ma, who loved the limelight, Pony Ma was incredibly media-shy. Pony gave his first interview to a foreign journalist in 2011, thirteen years after founding Tencent. He kept his family and life private and believed in action over flowery words. As a result, Tencent as a company followed Pony's example. One consequence of this reluctance to engage the media was that Tencent, the fourth most valuable company globally, has remained virtually unknown to the Western world.

Allen was as averse to the public eye as Pony, although it would be difficult to describe Allen as shy. He avoided talking to the media and was appalled at the idea of conferring with potential business partners who continuously knocked on WeChat's doors. However, once or twice a year, Allen would take the stage. In thoughtful marathon monologues in front of a packed audience, Allen would share his insights about WeChat and his philosophy on creating good products. These monologues could continue for up to eight hours.

Allen's slow and considered speaking style, along with his dislike of frivolous conversation, often led people to believe he was an anxious introvert. In one of the open talks, he addressed this: "People say I'm nervous. [Pause] I'm not nervous." Each day Allen would arrive at WeChat's building alone and dressed casually. With his head down he would make a beeline for his office in the far corner of WeChat's main building. There would be a continuous line of employees at his door, knowing he preferred to speak with people in the comfort of his own office and attempting to appear casual as they queued for his attention.

Allen and Pony were a match professionally and personally. The two always seemed to have great respect for one another. Both men developed messaging products that completely dominated the Chinese market. So when Tencent bought Foxmail, Pony was very eager to take Allen on board as well. Allen would continue to maintain Foxmail with his original team and became the head director of QQ mail. Pony hoped Allen could work his magic in email and turn his flailing QQ email service around.

Sure enough, under this new leadership, QQ mail flourished. Allen's first priority was to make the program lighter and faster, meaning it was easier to download, quicker to install, and smoother to operate. He then stripped the program back to its primary email function. Finally, he removed many superfluous bells and whistles likely included during Tencent's prolific ecosystem-building phase. After one year, QQ mail surpassed 10 million users, ten times the previous year's count. In 2009, QQ mail had 50 million users. By 2010, with the addition of "message in a bottle," a function that allowed users to send a message to any stranger willing to listen, QQ mail surpassed 100 million users. It had become the most popular email service in China. With that success, the Tencent ecosystem was more resilient than ever. (Jianshu, 2016)

The Smartphone Era

With the release of the first iPhone in 2007, and smartphone use growing exponentially beginning in 2009, the tech landscape shifted dramatically. The smartphone era had arrived, and this represented a new challenge and opportunity for Tencent.

Smartphones were an entirely new way to interact with the internet and digital services. Many existing tech firms struggled to adapt. As previously discussed, Facebook famously had to close its doors for a time to address the company's delayed mobile adaptation. They had optimized their code, platform, and user interface for the desktop web browser, which rendered the mobile experience slow and unwieldy. Later, Mark Zuckerberg would admit, "We took a bad bet." Fortunately, Facebook's timely and successful strategic overhaul helped them reap the rewards of the mobile revolution. (Wagner, 2019)

Tencent approached the smartphone revolution differently. Instead of overhauling QQ and other products to become mobile-optimized, Tencent decided to start from scratch. They created new products that would compete with their existing ones for mobile-user market share. This unique cannibalistic strategy allowed Tencent to beat itself before its competitors could do so. This internal competition didn't just pit product against product. It manifested itself amongst the teams themselves. Tencent would commonly allow half a dozen groups to simultaneously work on a project, with one eventually gaining sufficient momentum and resources to represent the entire company. This internal pressure and competition enabled the grassroots innovation that would ultimately give rise to WeChat.

WeChat's Humble Beginnings

In 2010, when smartphone adoption rates were exploding worldwide, several teams in Tencent simultaneously began developing mobile instant messenger (IM) apps. Allen Zhang, the founder of Foxmail and head of QQmail, created WeChat as his contribution. It quickly emerged as the most potent Tencent product. Allen had previously solved Tencent's big email service problem. It looked as though he would also be the one to overcome their next major challenge, that of maintaining social dominance on the smartphone.

The process began with news of Kik, a Canadian instant messaging (IM) app that had launched in October 2010 and gained one million registered users in its first 15 days. Learning of this unprecedented growth, Allen understood the disruption potential to QQ and Tencent's ecosystem. After a few back-and-forth sessions with Pony Ma, Allen received the green light to develop an IM app for Tencent. The WeChat project officially began on November 19, 2010. Allen and a small team created the first version, and in January 2011, WeChat (微信) formally came online.

Later, Allen and his team said their inspiration was primarily from Kik, with WeChat becoming the "Kik of the East." Ironically, five years later, Tencent bought a 5% share in Kik. Its founder Ted Livingston said, "Kik is the WeChat of the West." No matter who was copying whom, WeChat certainly had the right recipe for the Chinese market.

However, it wasn't a smooth start. In the first few months, WeChat endured an abysmal growth rate of approximately one thousand users per day. In addition, similar products were being launched in China with more substantial initial success, leading many internal team members to question the project's direction. Allen said the most challenging part was listening to people complain. The project "didn't make sense because everything WeChat was attempting to do could be done with mobile QQ ... they had no advantages and therefore no future." (Zheng & Xu, 2013)

So how did one product with "no future" go on to become the jewel in Tencent's heavily encrusted crown? It was due to initial creative developments that fostered early growth and virality.

11

GROWTH

WECHAT captured the tech world's attention with its phenomenal market valuation and monetization features. Yet, not of these existed in the beginning. The WeChat story has been one of gradual iteration. After it's creation, I put WeChat's story into four main phases: viral growth, bringing on businesses, monetizing, and creating an efficient ecosystem with mini programs. The next four chapters are broken into these four phases telling WeChat's

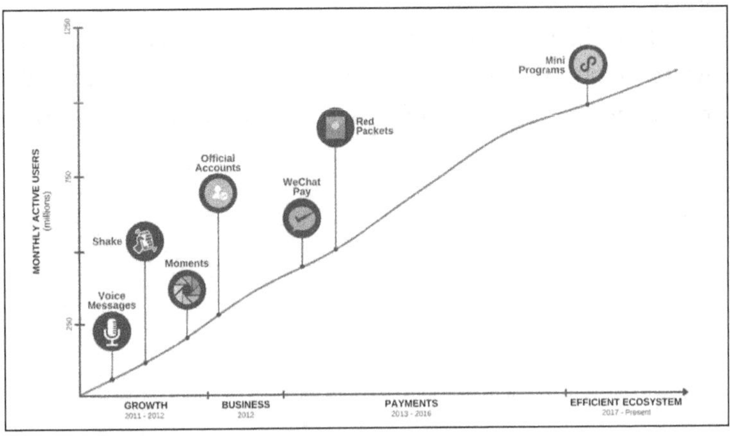

Figure 5: The WeChat Story.

As the number of users grew, so did WeChat. The app gained new features in thematic phases. First WeChat focused on growth, then businesses, then payments, and lastly created efficiency in the ecosystem with mini programs.

coming-of-age story.

None of WeChat's story could have happened without the initial user growth. Counterintuitively, WeChat's real value was created with a tiny team in these first several months. The critical growth phase. Only once WeChat had user traffic could it monetize, and only with user traffic could WeChat attract the thousands of businesses and services which make it a Superapp and cause it to be so valuable. Users must come first. Despite this fact, WeChat's all-important growth phase is not well known and often overlooked.

Three early developments contributed to WeChat's viral growth. Chronologically, these developments were the voice message function, unique ways to connect to strangers, and integrating messaging and social networking services (SNS).

The Voice Message Function

In April 2011, WeChat was inspired by another success story. TalkBox, a voice messaging app from Hong Kong, hit China by storm. It launched on January 18, 2011, and gained one million users in its first month. Three months in, and TalkBox was a mini phenomenon, having established a significant base of high-end, trendsetting users in Mainland China. Other messaging apps followed suit, with WeChat's competitor 米聊 or "Mi Talk" by XiaoMi quickly adding a voice message function.

Allen thought highly of the voice message functionality and pushed his team to integrate voice messaging into WeChat. On May 10, 2011, WeChat released version 2.0 with a voice message function and quickly saw a boost in user activity and acquisition of new users. While traditional text messages still constituted the bulk of user interaction, the novelty of voice messaging functionality attracted new users. Harvey Zhou, WeChat's then Assistant General Manager, reflected that "voice messaging

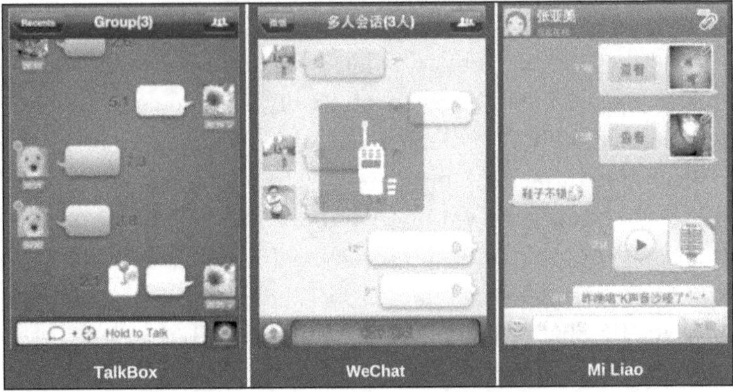

Figure 6: Voice Messaging in Chat Apps in 2011.

TalkBox (left) first provided voice messaging functionality which became popular amongst Chinese. Several months later WeChat and Mi Liao followed TalkBox's example. (Zhihu, 2019) (Soho, 2021)

wasn't an especially large portion of gross information flow, but many users would come [to WeChat] to give the function a try, they would then establish a relationship with the system and continue to use it." (Zheng & Xu, 2013)

There has been much speculation about why voice message functionality in China was much more popular than in other parts of the world. Some speculate that Chinese is more complex and slower to type than English or other languages. However, a university study in 2017 showed negligible differences in typing speeds, which disproved that theory. (Ruan, Wobbrock, Liou, Ng, & Landay, 2018) Others have speculated that Chinese people preferred voice messages because of an inability to read. Still, China has a high literacy rate of over 96%, so that theory is wrong, too.

I believe the Chinese love of voice messaging derives from China's language diversity, especially spoken language. China has hundreds of languages and even more dialects that can all be broken into multiple language groups. The most popular is the North China language group, with 1.2 billion native speakers in

Mandarin and many other related dialects. However, there are dozens of variants with a wide variety of pronunciations of the core Mandarin dialect, which is today the national language of China.

Perhaps the best way to understand China's linguistic diversity is with the phrase "每个地方都有地方话" or "every place has its own local dialect." Each social group has developed unique dialects throughout China's extensive history to communicate their culture and social norms. Local nuance is retained in verbal communication but lost in the written script, which is considered relatively formal and sterile. Therefore, it is no surprise that voice messages became incredibly popular on social platforms, where users were interacting with friends and family. They enabled a degree of intimacy and complexity that was simply lost in text. WeChat boosted its user base while taking advantage of a unique Chinese language characteristic by incorporating this functionality.

Connecting Strangers

By mid-2011, WeChat was seeing a user boost, but fierce industry competition meant it wasn't enough. So, while WeChat started as a tool for connecting friends and family, subsequent developments focused more on connecting strangers. This would contribute to the product's "positive network externality" and lead to industry dominance in China.

Positive network externality is where the value of a product increases with the more people who use it. Telephones are a good example. If billions of people have a telephone, it can connect to billions of people. On the other hand, if only one person in the world has it, the telephone is useless. Network effects are especially powerful for communication products like WeChat, which can engage a critical mass of users. This critical mass

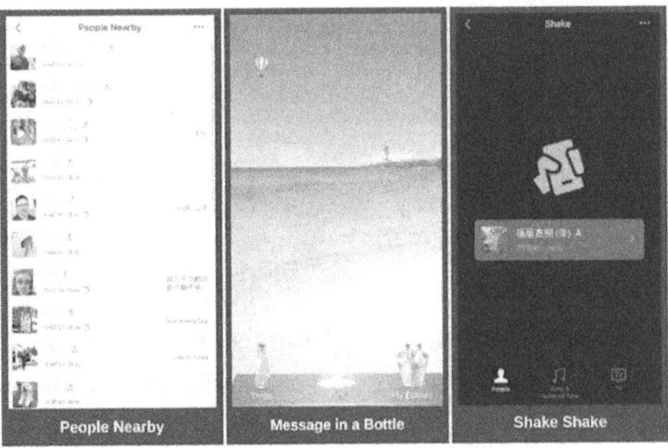

Figure 7: Connecting Strangers.

WeChat released these three prominent features to help strangers connect on the platform. (Message in a Bottle from Dial, 2013; Others by author)

ensures the rate of adoption becomes self-sustaining and creates further growth. Products with a solid social component each race to reach this critical mass, becoming the market standard.

To reach this coveted place, in late 2011, WeChat released three new features; People Nearby, Message in a Bottle, and Shake-Shake. These features had the common goal of connecting strangers - enabling users to easily add new friends beyond the traditional method of knowing and searching a user's phone number or WeChat ID. The first feature, released on August 3, with version 2.5, was People Nearby. This allowed users to see the profile, username, personal slogan, and distance to other geographically-close WeChat users. In addition, it included an option to filter by gender. A user could then send a simple greeting. If he or she received a reply, a conversation with a digital neighbor could ensue.

The next feature, Message in a Bottle, was borrowed directly from QQ Mail. A user would send out a message 'in a bottle' and then another user could 'pick up' the bottle and read or listen to the message. Users could send and receive messages to and from the ether – they could interact with one another whilst maintaining complete anonymity.

The third feature would become WeChat's most iconic. The Shake-Shake feature was an entirely new innovation based on the concept of making a smartphone and WeChat an extension of one's hand. The original inspiration came from a simple app called Bump, which allowed users to literally bump smartphones and exchange contacts and photos. Allen wanted to help WeChat users connect similarly while expanding beyond nearby users. The Shake-Shake feature allowed users to shake their phone and see a list of other users organized by distance who were also shaking. A table of friends finishing dinner and all shaking their phones became a common sight in China. This fist shaking movement became quintessentially "WeChat."

Within WeChat and the broader Chinese tech world, many speak of the "loser strategy." The saying goes, "得屌丝，得天下," "get the losers, get the world." Chinese product managers believe that a type of functionality that is attractive to a "loser" will end up attracting everyone. In the three months following July 2011, WeChat had released three features that embodied this strategy. Gimmicky functions were included that allowed the proverbial "loser" to connect with strangers and decrease social isolation. Then, it is no surprise that Allen Zhang unabashedly drew comparisons between the Shake-Shake feature and the pleasure derived from relieving loneliness.

Near the end of 2011, on 20 December, WeChat launched an English version. The 3.5 software update added the QR code function. QR codes allowed users to generate a personalized matrix image that others could scan in person, online, or in print to add an individual as a friend. This removed the real-time connection barrier. Users were no longer required to be online to send and receive friend requests. Over time, WeChat continued to incorporate functions from launching websites to triggering payment transactions that utilized QR codes. This release began a new trend that bridged offline encounters to online interactions.

Shu Shen Lu (陆树燊), a member of WeChat's founding team, explained that the WeChat versions "from 2.1 to 3.5, were just to achieve one thing: allow users to constantly add new friends." (Lu, 2018) The focus on viral network externality worked, and in March 2012, WeChat reached 100 million registered users. It took WeChat 15 months to achieve this milestone, whereas Facebook and Twitter took 54 months and 49 months, respectively. WeChat had succeeded. It had reached critical mass and become the industry standard.

Completing the Social Ecosystem

Now that the odds seemed to be tipping significantly in WeChat's favor, it was time to shift its core product strategies away from their focus on user acquisition. Instead, WeChat would now develop features that deepened the interaction between existing users. They achieved this with the groundbreaking integration of messaging and social networking services (SNS).

Most digital programs that connect people can be placed into one of two categories within the context of social media:

- Real-time communication tools, which includes ICQ, AIM, QQ, MSN Messenger, and Skype
- SNS, which include Friendster, Myspace, and Facebook.

No product, prior to WeChat, had successfully bridged these two categories. Even Facebook didn't have good messaging user experience until releasing stand-alone app, called "Messenger", focused on messaging in August 2011, and gradually improving the functionality.

On April 19, 2012, WeChat changed this status quo by releasing Moments with version 4.0. Lyle Chen (陈岳伟), a WeChat founding developer and later head of WeChat's iOS front-end development, said they had considered releasing an earlier simpler version. "But in the end, we all agreed, it'd be better to release a version which would shock the industry." (Zheng & Xu, 2013) The Moments function allowed users to share photos and notes on a timeline with their friends, who can then like and leave comments. The home page of Moments was a newsfeed in which users could see updates from friends. With the advent of Moments, WeChat had boldly done what no other social media had successfully done before and became both a communication tool and an SNS.

The original impetus behind the new functionality was to revitalize the relationships among WeChat users. Moments became an icebreaker by providing personalized conversation fodder for users and their now extensive networks. For example, a comment on someone's hat posted on Moments could reignite an old friendship.

Genie Lin, Senior Product Manager at WeChat, reflected on this uncharted territory. "I felt very anxious because there was no benchmark to learn from. We developed this product for 3 to 4 months, sometimes we felt very excited ... sometimes we felt that we couldn't grasp the critical points." (Zheng & Xu, 2013) At WeChat, Genie was essentially the second in charge of product development. While all final product decisions were made by Allen Zhang, they first had to pass her review. Because the team was not sure how successful Moments would be, the new feature was hidden in the "Friends" submenu (later named "Discover"). This soft launch technique was a tactic that WeChat would continue to use for new functions.

Initially, the apprehension around Moments was justified. In the first six months, the adoption rate was low. Many in the industry were pessimistic about the new feature, in part because of the fierce competition from China's micro-blogging giant, Weibo, a product with similar features Twitter.

However, 2012 saw Weibo's popularity drop. Users increasingly disliked its impersonal style of communication. They said that it had become a vanity fair, with everyone shouting and no one listening. Users turned to WeChat because it felt more personal and more authentic.

Later that year Moments became a hit. WeChat's users were in the hundreds of millions and most were posting their life updates to Moments. The new feature had launched at a perfect time when Chinese users were looking for more genuine and personal interactions at a public level. WeChat had achieved the previously impossible, successfully combining the two main categories of social media, SNS and real-time communications (comms), into one.

Facebook still struggles with bridging these categories today. Facebook and Messenger, which represent the categories of SNS and comms respectively, have a poorly integrated experience. Users jump back and forth between apps providing a jolting and confusing experience. By comparison, WeChat's Moments and WeChat's chat functions provide a seamless experience in one app, which continues to flourish today. Of WeChat's 1.2 billion active users, 750 million users are using Moments daily, the average user accessing Moments ten times a day.

By successfully combining two separate social media categories, WeChat had taken its first steps to becoming a superapp. Furthermore, the voice messaging feature was a hit with Chinese, and three key viral growth features were connecting strangers and friends quickly and easily on the app to quickly grow users and their number of connections on the app. WeChat was fast becoming an integral part of the Chinese digital lifestyle.

Now that WeChat had successfully engaged individuals, user quantity was hitting critical mass and gaining steam, the logical next step was to focus on businesses. WeChat wanted to bring businesses into the ecosystem to give users content to engage with, and begin setting the foundations for methods of monetization in the future.

12

Connecting Business

As WeChat had grown and expanded the functionality of existing user-to-user connections, it was time to bring businesses and content creators onto the platform. So, in late 2012, WeChat began releasing multiple functions that brought two primary benefits to its ecosystem. These were increased user value and reliable sources of monetization. This began the WeChat transition from a program to a platform, a distinction it would continue to develop until it established itself as China's go-to digital ecosystem.

User Value

After pivoting from user growth to user interaction, WeChat continued to broaden its value to existing consumers. To do so, WeChat introduced Official Accounts and the Game Center, which connected users directly to information and entertainment. Gone were the days when WeChat was just another messaging tool.

On August 23, 2012, WeChat introduced the Official Account Platform. This feature enabled third-party developers to connect business Customer Relationship Management (CRM) systems directly to WeChat. In addition, it made it possible to attach Application Programming Interfaces (API) and provide an entire range of customizable tools and services to its users.

Figure 8: An Official Account.

A Chamber of Commerce welcomes a new follower.

The accounts themselves looked like business-centric WeChat users that individuals could follow to access regular announcements, web shortcuts, company contact cards, and much more, see.

Companies now had a home on China's most popular digital platform. However, WeChat didn't stop there. It also opened the platform to smaller content creators. Two types of Official Accounts, services, and subscriptions were created. The service account was reserved for larger companies with a business license; it functioned like a WeChat company landing page. The subscription type could be opened by individuals and didn't require a business license. It focused on written article updates; effectively, it behaved like a WeChat blog space or news site. Any Official Accounts to which a user subscribed were located within their Chats tab, which meant that their opt-in information and news were co-located amongst friends' conversations.

WeChat enacted strict rules within the Official Account platform, with the primary goal of cultivating user value. The rules encouraged businesses to compete fairly and disincentivized bad behavior such as coercing users into sharing content for prizes that would degrade interpersonal relationships and platform authenticity. Such behavior could start a negative cycle that would and compromise the health and longevity of the platform. The intent was to ensure that only 'good' content and valuable services could become viral within WeChat. In other words, the only way to succeed was to bring value to WeChat users. This, in turn, would make WeChat more valuable to users.

Official Accounts were a huge success and saw many companies, media outlets, celebrities, and specialty bloggers joining in to make content. By August 2015, three years after its launch, the number of WeChat Official Accounts had surpassed 10 million.

Monetization

Now that WeChat had a thriving platform of users and businesses, it needed to start making money. Unlike most Western social media that solely monetize through ads, Tencent has traditionally taken a more varied approach; testing out different techniques and seeing what users like. WeChat was no exception. Allen Zhang was especially wary of monetization degrading the user experience. In version 5.0, WeChat released four new features focused on monetization. The Games Center, the Sticker Market, digital advertising and WeChat Pay.

The Games Center added a social element to mobile gaming and created a unified place to launch games. Users could play simple web-based games within the center or launch their favorite Tencent games apps (downloaded separately) and login with their WeChat credentials. This allowed users to more easily find and play with their WeChat friends and compare score rankings. The next year, Tencent became the world's largest video game publisher by revenue with significant investments in game companies overseas. (Newzoo, 2014)

Connecting WeChat to these games lowered the playing barrier to entry. Users could instantly see what games their friends had played and the scoreboard for their entire network. The personalization enabled certain games to become viral by introducing them through friends to new players and encouraging friendly competition. This was a technique that WeChat would fully leverage over the coming years.

The Games Center helped push traffic to Tencent's gaming ecosystem, while the integration with WeChat Pay made in-game purchases even easier. Socially-focused games benefited the most from WeChat integration. In particular, Tencent's Arena of Valor benefited from the synergy and went viral. Arena of Valor is a mobile MoBA – a "Multiplayer online Battle Arena" is a social game where two teams of five players battle head-to-head – that grossed US$6.7 billion from 2016 to 2019, becoming one of the highest-grossing mobile games of all time.

During this time, WeChat also experimented with a paid sticker market. This sticker model had proved highly profitable for chatting apps in other Asian countries, namely Japan's Line and South Korea's KakaoTalk, which dominate their respective markets. Both products had shown an impressive ability to monetize intellectual property (IP) from their own sticker content, as well as that created by independent artists. Stickers were small visual images supported in-app, rather than as an attachment, which users could send instead of words. The idea was to attract high-level artists, companies, and celebrities to develop exclusive content for the platform. This led to WeChat signing partnerships with Disney and Pixar, among other creative companies. However, in the end, Chinese people were less willing to pay for this content than their Japanese and South Korean counterparts. As a result, while WeChat's Sticker Market did liven up the platform, it did not become a strong source of revenue.

The third feature was traditional paid advertising. Allen Zhang was particularly apprehensive that ads would degrade WeChat's user experience and was very careful and restrictive in the manner in which ads were implemented. To reflect this mindset, WeChat Ads slogan is "ads can also be a part of a lifestyle". The first batch of ads was by invitation only with a handful of brands including BMW and Coca-cola to ensure quality and control. The ads were displayed on WeChat Moments, which still remain WeChat's main advertising real estate. While WeChat has opened up Moments ads to the public, they still maintain many restrictions to maintain user experience, these include a minimum ¥50,000 CNY (USD ~8,000 USD) ad spend and limiting total number of ads a user sees to three per day – the average Facebook user sees hundreds.

The fourth monetization strategy was WeChat Pay. This new feature went well beyond revenue generation and created value on the platform unlike any digital application before. It was one of WeChat's major steps to becoming a superapp and requires a chapter of its own.

13

PAYMENT

NOTHING CHANGED the entire industry as much as adding payment functionality with WeChat Pay. WeChat Pay allowed users to connect their bank accounts and send money to friends or to companies as they purchase goods or services. WeChat's social prowess and sheer convenience made WeChat Pay a major success. In 2014, Alipay, the first-mover that launched a decade earlier, had a whopping 82% of the mobile payment market while WeChat Pay had 10%. Two years later, WeChat Pay had wrestled 40% of the market, and Alipay's share was down to 54%. (iResearch, 2015; iResearch, 2017)

This late-game success was due primarily to three new features that increased the coverage of digital payment: Red Packets, QR code P2P (peer-to-peer) payment, and Official Account (OA) payment between consumers and businesses.

Red Packets

By far, the single most significant contributor to WeChat Pay's success was the introduction of Red Packets, which was an innovative marriage of social interaction and finance that allowed users to gift money to their friends. It leveraged China's culture of gifting and history of festive celebrations, as well as

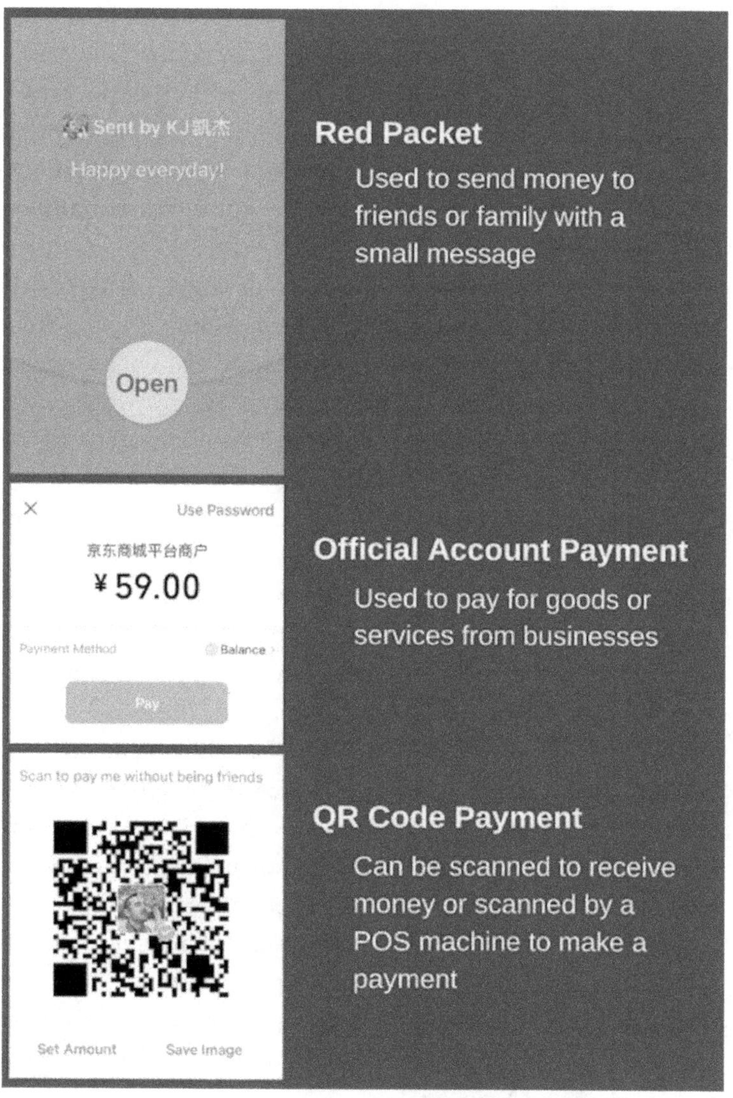

Figure 9: The Three Primary Payments.

WeChat's unique social advantage over competitors like Alipay.

The gifting of red packets is an old cultural tradition across the Chinese diaspora worldwide. In the modern-day, Chinese gift money within a red envelope on Chinese New Year (Spring festival), weddings, birthdays, and other festive celebrations. When the Western tradition dictated a gift, Chinese tradition offered a Red Packet.

WeChat first entertained the idea of digital red packets internally within Tencent in 2014. After a warm reception from employees and iterative testing, WeChat officially released the Red Packet functionality on January 20, 2015, with version 6.1. The feature was located in the app's most significant entry point, the main chat window.

The launch corresponded with China's most important holiday, the Chinese New Year. It was promoted on Chinese New Year Eve, a new year countdown TV program, a modern Chinese phenomenon with viewership second only to the US Superbowl. Partnering with brands across China, the promotion prompted viewers to use the Shake-Shake function and receive a Red Packet gift. In one night, around 500 million yuan (US$70 million) in cash and 3 billion yuan (US$423 million) in coupons were gifted to users. The launch was a huge success and saw users sending Red Packets directly to their friends far beyond the original promotion. Within two weeks of Red Packets' debut, approximately 1 billion Red Packets were sent in a single day. In 2015, WeChat's Red Packets became a part of Chinese daily life. Over time, the number sent out by users every day gradually increased, with spikes on holidays like Mid-Autumn Festival and International New Year's.

Chinese New Year Red Packet gifting spiked again in 2016, with users sending 8 billion gifts in a single night. The following year, that number was hit 14 billion. WeChat Pay saw this evolve

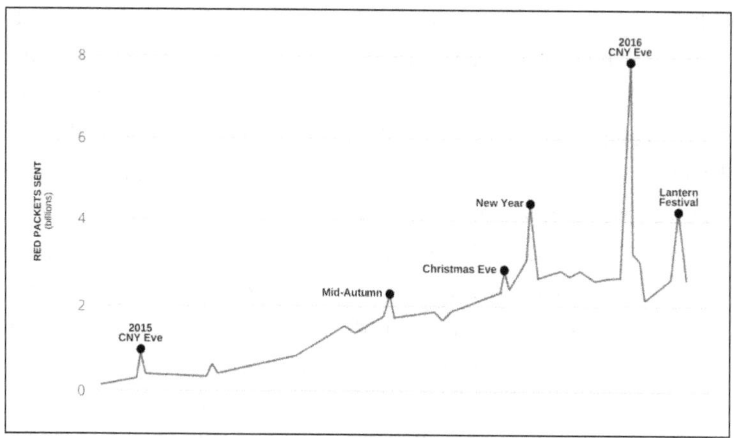

Figure 10: Red Packets Sent per Day.

Red packet gifting spiked around holidays which would raise the subsequent gifting average. CNY created the most prominent spikes. (Chao, 2017)

into a regular trend. The Chinese New Year brings a new spike in the number of Red Packets sent in a single day every year. After that, the daily average would continue to be higher than it was before the spike. Within WeChat, this phenomenon was called 'raising the peak value,' where the daily average of Red Packets sent was permanently increased after reaching new heights from a viral campaign or holiday event. This daily average increased would be due to the viral event gaining new adopters or existing users changing their daily habits after a 24-hour Red Packet frenzy.

QR Code Payment

After users had joined WeChat Pay to access novelty benefits like Red Packets, they were encouraged to continue sending and receiving money using a personalized QR code that could be accessed by any other user. This meant users no longer needed to be friends to conduct a financial transaction.

WeChat had already normalized this technology through

QR code-enabled friend requests facilitated by a built-in code scanner. The fact that virtually everyone in China had a personal WeChat account meant virtually no barriers impeded individuals from exchanging money. Small, off-the-books services could also be transacted with unique QR codes, effectively establishing a digital cash-in-hand economy.

However, a sizable segment of small businesses wanted additional security and legitimacy with their QR code payments but didn't want to go through the process of registering for an Official Account. This necessitated creating an option to pay directly to a business rather than an individual using a QR code. WeChat facilitated this distinction by enabling independent developers to create QR codes linking directly to third-party payment platforms.

These third-party platforms, like Youzan, allowed businesses to receive payment via WeChat Pay, Alipay, or other payment tools from a single merchant page. This segment grew overtime as QR code payments gained more traction and needed to be less of a gray market. Soon, payment QR codes were available everywhere. Users could scan to pay taxi drivers, local food markets, street food vendors, and infamously, even some beggars, just by scanning their QR code. Anyone and everyone had a way to pay. Convenience had become WeChat Pay's mainstay.

Official Account Payment

Businesses that registered for an Official Account could generate official QR codes for payment and take advantage of closed-loop ecommerce – the ability to market and sell goods and services in the same place. Payment-enabled Official Accounts meant users could see, purchase, and recommend a product to their friends within the WeChat ecosystem. A purchasing experience like this was unprecedented.

However, accessing this functionality wasn't a simple task. Payment functionality was only available for service-type Official Accounts. In contrast, subscription types were still reserved solely for information, blogging, and news. To register, companies had to provide a copy of their business license, link their business bank account, and complete many regulatory verifications.

Once online, businesses had the luxury of a custom WeChat landing page with built-in purchasing capabilities. Companies could collect big data and observe customer transaction patterns from a single platform. In addition, they could use coupons and discounts sent via their Official Account directly to users to spur more activity. WeChat had successfully enabled users to access digital goods and services from within WeChat via ecommerce websites. These were similar to Shopify's ecommerce sites in the West, but optimized for WeChat. I recall using one such ecommerce website to purchasing tickets to a running marathon. After buying a ticket, I could send a customized link to friends who could then easily join my same running group and purchase a ticket. This type of purchase took full advantage of WeChat's social prowess and enabled viral ecommerce.

With the high adoption of WeChat Pay, and the new value created by the entire ecosystem, WeChat functioned seamlessly and grew for three solid years. Users could purchase and execute hundreds of thousands of services. It was at this time, circa 2016, that first arose mentions of 'WeChat' and 'Superapp' in the West by the tech-savvy who were realizing the capability of the platform.

However, as ecommerce websites became more complex, they were hampered by the Official Account HTML framework. This somewhat antiquated coding language was as old as the web, making large shopping pages clunky and unstable. As a result, users gravitated to specialized ecommerce platforms like TMall, TaoBao, and JD.com, which offered a smoother online shopping experience. WeChat Pay had caught up to the competition by optimizing payment across their platform with Red Packets, QR codes, and Official Account ecommerce, but they hit a tech-based bottleneck. It was time to shock the industry again.

14

Mini Programs

In early 2017, WeChat released "mini programs." Mini programs are like mini apps within WeChat that users don't have to download. They have functionality just shy of a fully-developed application but are accessed just as easily as opening a webpage. No installation required. The advent of mini programs solidified WeChat's position as the world's first Superapp.

Mini programs increased WeChat's efficiency for businesses, developers, and users, strengthening its closed-loop ecosystem. In addition, where WeChat had previously been transformed from messaging platform to tool, mini programs saw it now expand from an app to an operating environment.

The Efficiency Challenge

There were two challenges, one technical and the other user-centric, that WeChat's mini programs sought to overcome. Both required that WeChat improve its efficiency.

Technically, WeChat's platform capacity was based on websites using HTML code. This mature technology used since the beginning of the web is flexible but lacked the power to support modern-day functionality. To continue on the earlier example, buying tickets for a marathon involved entering multiple layers of personal information before paying. While going page to page the website might crash or the information you entered would disappear. You'd have to try multiple times before successfully buying the service or product you wanted. While businesses liked Official Accounts (OAs) and their closed-loop capability, users were getting annoyed at the instability and limitations of basic web-browser ecommerce.

For many organizations, including bloggers, news agencies, and celebrities, OAs were enough. They only wanted the marketing and content creation capability. These entities had no need for complex back-end systems or multi-layered ecommerce capabilities. For these media-related organizations, OAs currently functionality, but businesses and developers who wanted more complex and efficient interactions wanted to do more.

By traditional measures, WeChat had an incredible user experience. An average user was spending approximately 90 minutes per day on WeChat– Facebook average usage, by comparison, was 38 minutes per day. (He, 2019) WeChat was the envy of Silicon Valley and the darling of investors; longer usage time meant more user traffic, and more user traffic meant more money. However, Allen saw this as a sign of low efficiency. He believed users were getting stuck on WeChat. In a 2017 internal talk, Allen described WeChat as a tool; the faster a user could accomplish a task, the better. He used a physical tool as a comparison; a hammer that could pound in a nail in five seconds was better than a hammer that could do it in five minutes. He equated long usage time to slow capacity. Rather than time spent in-app, WeChat should measure its success by the amount of user value created within a given amount of time. In short, WeChat needed a way to efficiently deliver a high-value user experience.

The Mini Program Solution

Before WeChat's mini programs, no widely used product

Figure 11: Placing Mini Program.

Mini Program is a new type of simple mobile program sitting between a website and an app.

spanned the gap between a website and an app for almost a decade. WeChat mini programs are light mobile applications produced by developers with functionality on the continuum between a website and an app. They work exclusively within WeChat. One could describe them as either its super-powerful, mobile-friendly websites or stripped-down apps.

Much like Official Account functionality, WeChat provided the platform for mini programs to allow businesses to engage third-party developers to create real solutions. Many technical benefits came with the mini program platform rules and requirements. A two-megabyte limit was imposed, so there was no installation or application management needed, which meant mini programs had a low barrier to entry for users.

With mini programs, Allen Zhang said he aimed to accomplish a dream as old as the creation of the internet. Mini programs had strict rules prohibiting excessive follow-ups or notifications prodding users. He explained that users could "use it and walk away" (用完即走). He wanted a product platform where users could quickly accomplish their goal and walk away unhindered, similar to the original philosophy of websites but with new modern functionality and efficiency.

Mini programs were built using Tencent's own coding

language based on Javascript, facilitating rapid development. Javascript supports object-oriented and functional programming, enabling complex interactions within a much more stable user experience. Mini programs were also native to WeChat, meaning they could be shared to direct chats, searched, favorited, accessed via QR code, and much more.

The Overall Benefits

The benefits of adding mini program functionality to the WeChat platform included improved eCommerce, an optimized WeChat ecosystem, and tighter controls on businesses and developers.

Ecommerce

Mini programs allowed WeChat to contend with ecommerce competitors. It offered businesses something other platforms lacked, which was customizability. Brands could leverage the blank canvas provided by the mini program framework. On Tmall, Taobao, JD.com, etc., it was difficult for brands and products to differentiate themselves. These platforms were designed as mass marketplaces, prioritizing product display consistency over branding. That meant it was easy to filter everyday commodities and find the most value for money. However, for branded items, it was often hard to distinguish genuine from fake.

The mini program returned design autonomy to the business, which meant that it offered both purchasing and marketing capabilities. This gave brands greater control over their ecommerce decreasing the likelihood of fakes and the direction communication of consumer to brand increased the feeling of authenticity. Consumer-facing businesses with strong brands especially liked this new functionality. Tesla, for example, made a mini program enabling users to buy a Tesla car, locate charging stations, and learn about Tesla.

Optimizing the WeChat Ecosystem

Prior to the advent of mini programs, users purchased goods and services on WeChat via websites linked to Official Accounts. However, these were cumbersome and offered a poor user experience. Mini programs rectified this issue with native app experience and stabilized digital retail transactions between users and brands. For example, a user could learn about a product from a friend, buy it with WeChat Pay, and share their home address for shipping. If the product was referred to a friend, the cycle was repeated.

Virtually everything that was once accomplished with websites could now be done by more streamlined mini programs, making WeChat a more efficient and valuable tool. Furthermore, with all this functionality within one app, linked payment, and a large user base, WeChat's ecosystem was naturally broadened and strengthened.

In addition, a competitor would have great difficulty replicating this ecosystem because of positive network externality effects. To provide a platform which competed with WeChat, a competitor would need to attract twenty million businesses to provide valuable transactions and content, attract 1.2 billion users, convince 80% of users to link their bank cards, and incentivize all those individuals to use the platform nearly every day.

Tighter Controls

Mini programs also included a new set of rules supported by increased due diligence from WeChat. Like apps on Android and iOS, mini programs and their future updates had to be approved by the system administrator, WeChat. Before this, WeChat content creation was more open, with Official Accounts edited on mobile-friendly 'back-end' websites with minimal surveillance.

Unfortunately, this laxity resulted in myriad uncouth industry practices. These ranged from phishing schemes and misleading UI (User Interface) to promotions incentivizing users to repost content that devalued WeChat Moments. Mini programs, however, allowed WeChat to clean up content and standardize user experiences within the WeChat ecosystem.

Challenges to Success

The main challenges that mini programs faced were threefold: pitching it without any similar products to reference, navigating operating system fees, and requiring additional effort from businesses and developers.

Initially, it was challenging to get businesses to buy into the mini program concept. Unlike most innovations in China, mini programs were a true novelty. A significant problem was explaining the platform to companies and convincing them that it was advantageous to develop their own programs. Fortunately, WeChat was by far the market leader in multiple areas, and businesses were eager to remain relevant and up-to-date on market trends.

Additionally, WeChat was navigating the new territory of smartphone operating system fees. With Apple and Google developing their respective operating systems, iOS and Android, the two smartphones had a combined share of more than 98% of the smartphone operating system market. Both operating systems charged a 30% platform fee for app and in-app purchases, but mini programs were considered apps within an app, meaning that the classification was grey for any revenue generated on this new platform. Initially, WeChat avoided these fees by downplaying the value of mini programs and gradually introducing more complexity and functionality after the initial launch. Within Tencent, this "low-key" strategy is popular and commonly employed. However, in early 2019, Apple began to ask questions and demand revenue for what they saw as in-app purchases. (Chen & Tan, 2019)

Finally, mini programs also faced a challenge from the open customizability that set them apart. As with Official Accounts, WeChat didn't create the mini programs; they just provided the framework and building blocks. Development and platform integration had to be driven by businesses and third-party developers.

Success

In their first year, despite the various challenges, mini programs thrived. They generated industry copycats across many industries. One year after launch, there were 580,000 mini programs used by 170 million users each day online. More than 1 million software developers registered as mini program developers. WeChat's big gamble was successful and had changed the industry. By late 2018, other players, including Alipay, Baidu, and ByteDance were releasing their own version of mini programs within their respective ecosystems.

Mini Games

Just as mini programs were beginning to prove successful, WeChat released Mini Games. Previously, mini programs were restricted from making any gaming content. In mid-December 2017, WeChat released 15 Mini Games. "挑一挑" or "Jump jump" was incredibly successful, gaining 100 million daily active users in just two weeks. As WeChat Mini Games took off, it increased the popularity of mini programs in general. It became a critical new method of monetizing Tencent's vast gaming empire. Why were Mini Games so popular? Before Mini Games, the two media for mobile games were native app games and web-app games. Mini Games had low acquisition costs, making them far more shareable and viral than native app games. While web-app games might have similarly low acquisition costs, Mini Games had much better performance and provided an enhanced overall gaming experience.

15

Recent Trends and Direction

WeChat's introduction of mini programs was a crucial component in its evolution from messaging app to an operating system that supported its own closed-loop ecosystem. WeChat has made the transition from toy to tool. Where once people played WeChat, they are now using it. It has shifted from a lifestyle product to a work and utility product. This is its strategic advantage over other products and gives us insight into where the company is heading.

Historically, WeChat had strategically avoided becoming a work tool by creating its own independent professional platform, WeChat Work. However, despite this effort, an overwhelming majority of Chinese people use WeChat for work and networking. With the success of mini programs, people increasingly use WeChat for utility. As a testament to this, WeChat dropped some of its initial features like Message in a Bottle in 2019.

As WeChat becomes more of a work and utility tool, the Chinese are finding new places to play. 2018 and 2019 saw a massive drop in WeChat user traffic on the Official Accounts platform as users shifted to more exciting and dynamic content like ByteDance's TouTiao and Douyin (TikTok's China-version). Allen Zhang responded to this at the beginning of 2019 by committing the year to focus on photo and video content. As a result, WeChat released Time Capsule, an ephemeral short video format, and several other small functions without minimal user uptake. However, in 2022, WeChat seems to have found the correct feature to combat Douyin, its own short-video platform within the WeChat app called Channels.

WeChat Channels looks very similar to other short-video platforms such as Douyin and Kuaishou, but with significant differences. These differences take advantage of WeChat as the center of China's social ecosystem. By default, Channels recommends content based on that which a user's friends view and like. This is in contrast to the AI/machine learning algorithm that Bytedance says powers the stickiness – that is, the length of time a user engages with an application – of Douyin. While Douyin and Kuaishou still dominate the short-video market, by 2022, WeChat Channels had already gained 400 million daily active users (DAU).

In addition to the foray into the short-video market, WeChat has focused on its primary strength as a digital utility tool. It has cleaned up the existing Official Account platform by implementing new rules for promotional sharing, restrictions on group buying, and discouraging destructive user behavior. Better governance of its platform has improved both its content and user experience.

User experience continues to broaden as WeChat's capacity grows. A large part of this growth is attributed to the combination of WeChat Pay and mini programs. Purchases via WeChat mini programs in 2020 amounted to US$247 billion, doubling the previous year's numbers. WeChat mini programs and WeChat Pay, released in 2017 and 2014 respectively, were WeChat's saving grace and continue to be its most significant source of value.

WeChat has come a long way from its beginnings as a simple messaging app, growing in popularity with viral functions and SNS capacity. It has slowly built the capacity to house businesses, payment, and now fully functional mini apps within itself. WeChat has made a pivotal transition as its own operating system, which sustains a vast closed-loop ecosystem. In short, it has succeeded in becoming the world's first Superapp, people could achieve virtually all mobile services via the one app.

This is indicative of a shift that is occurring beyond the walls of WeChat. Throughout the China tech world, apps are conglomerating their functionality. The way users operate online is changing as well. This is what we call the new digital revolution. Examining its takeoff in China will help us understand what we can expect globally.

Part 3

The Payment-led Digital Revolution

An explosion of mobile payment and closed-loop systems heralds China's new digital revolution. In Part 3, we examine the elements influencing this revolution, offer predictions of what's next for WeChat and its competitor Alipay, and provide an analysis of the international payment market.

WeChat's innovation and success have put China at the forefront of a new digital revolution, changing the way we interact online and shifting from standalone activities to closed-loop systems. At the heart of these systems is mobile payment functionality.

China's digital payment revolution started early. Today, China's integration of mobile payment far surpasses that of the US and rest of the West. Understanding China's mobile payment boom is crucial for businesses looking to sell into the China market. It is also valuable for those interested in glimpsing the future of payment globally.

How did China become the frontrunner in a payment-led digital revolution? The same contextually specific elements that now limit Chinese companies from expanding beyond China provide the answer. This means that although Chinese companies, like Tencent, laid the foundations for an entirely new form of digital interaction, it is likely to be Western tech giants, like Google and Apple, that will dominate the mobile payment sector globally.

16

Mobile Payment and Closed-Loop Systems

Mobile payments are regulated transactions initiated from a mobile device. The two leading mobile payment types are P2P (Peer-to-Peer) payment or B2C (Business-to-Consumer. A P2P mobile payment scenario involves, for instance, digitally transferring money to a friend to pay them back for dinner. Paying a business (B2C) could be done offline by swiping your mobile device - instead of cash or card - at a brick-and-mortar shop or online by selecting a digital payment tool instead of PayPal (or something similar) at check-out instead of entering your credit card information.

China has fully adopted mobile payment via WeChat Pay and Alipay, catalyzing significant growth in their respective ecosystems. This is especially true for WeChat, which has already played an essential role in Chinese daily life. The advent of mobile payment has enabled WeChat to manifest a closed-loop system within which the entire consumer journey occurs.

Traditionally, the consumer journey has spanned dozens, sometimes hundreds of channels. Consumers become aware of products and services on TV, radio, or outdoor advertising. They learn more about products in magazines or by searching for information and reading online. Third, they purchase products in supermarkets or large retailers and physically return for re-

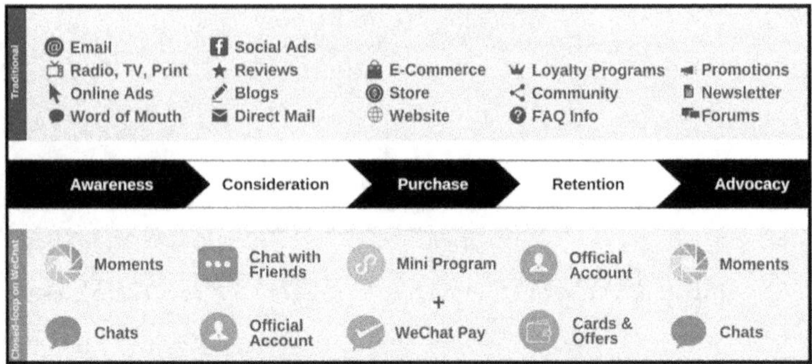

Figure 12: Traditional vs. Closed-Loop Systems.

Traditionally brands interacted with consumers over hundreds of distinct channels. Now brands can complete the consumer journey within one platform.

purchase. Lastly, online written reviews or chatting in-person provide recommendations that reinforce the buying cycle.

With WeChat, this entire journey can be accomplished without leaving the app. This is definitive of a closed-loop. A user reads articles and advertisements on products; researches and compares products; buys using mini programs; provides their delivery address; leaves a review, and makes recommendations to friends using chats or Moments. The cycle repeats itself - all without leaving WeChat.

Marketing teams love closed-loop systems. They can clearly and easily measure ROI (Return on Investment) for marketing campaigns. This was previously difficult to track across the multiple hundreds of varying interaction points with consumers. Now a user clicks on a business's ad, purchases the product, and then refers to a friend, who also purchases a product and then refers another first and so on and so forth. Businesses can know exactly how effective their marketing efforts are in generating real revenue, not just how many views or clicks they get.

Beyond the consumer journey, Tencent now have access to an unprecedented granularity of user data because many users do everything within the Tencent ecosystem. This cannot be done in the United States without consolidating and normalizing disparate database systems. Tencent executives have boasted that they can label individual behavior with over 5,000 discrete tags. This provides a near-perfect profile of each person and their interests based on actual behavior. Businesses can leverage data by buying highly targeted ads.

This all sounds scary for users, but they've benefitted too. The closed-loop system improves the user experience because it provides a quick and convenient way to accomplish virtually everything in one congruous environment. Much of WeChat's ecosystem is developed by third-parties. Similar to apps, WeChat mini programs undergo a stringent review process which requires approval from a WeChat appointed personnel. This ensures high-quality standards and good user experiences. As we shall see, several other vital components further enhance the closed-loop system.

Enhancing Closed-Loop Systems

Four key components enhance WeChat's closed-loop systems, making them even more powerful. These are the proliferation of savable user profiles, mini programs, practical application of AI, and well-integrated transitions between social and payment.

Saved user profiles have significantly lowered the barrier to executing transactions within WeChat. This allows users to utilize their information and preferences stored within WeChat and quickly share with businesses. For example, WeChat users can opt to 'share their home address instead of filling out an address. Auto-populating increases efficiency.

Mini programs allow businesses to provide users with a native-app experience without requiring them to download individual applications. This provides more sophisticated user interactions than websites with a much lower barrier to entry than an app. Mini programs power quick transactions, encourage follow-on purchases, and facilitate loyalty programs.

Artificial intelligence is gradually enhancing WeChat's closed-loop system. Users can obtain tailored solutions and instant responses to queries. Hybrids of AI combined with human customer service have become commonplace. Chatbots triage and accomplish simple tasks, while humans step-in to provide customer services that involve more complex queries.

Combining social interaction and mobile payment within a closed-loop system has propelled the ecosystem's overall value. A recommendation with a mini program link can create a new purchasing customer within seconds. The closed-loop system within a social ecosystem creates an environment where rapid purchasing is possible and viral sharing is facilitated.

Essential to creating the closed-loop system is mobile payment, which allows easy transactions between users and businesses. While the West's consumer culture has remained focused on credit and debit cards, China has skipped physical cards and the PC/desktop era and pioneered a payment-led digital revolution. To understand the full extent of this boom, one needs to look at the big numbers.

China's Mobile Payment Phenomenon

China's mobile payment numbers are truly staggering. In 2016 China's mobile payments already outpaced the US by a factor of 80. This gap was estimated to double with China's mobile payment transaction volume reaching US$45 trillion in 2021. In mobile payments, China has leapfrogged past the US. (Purnell, 2017; iResearch, 2021)

17

China's Mobile Payment Explosion

Four factors created the conditions for China's mobile payment miracle, generally reflecting the same four factors that led to China's own internet. Historically, China skipped desktop computers and 'plastic' banking cards, which now limit options for the developed world. Culturally, the Chinese view privacy and security concerns as frivolous and are happy to opt for convenience. Finally, China's government and business environment embrace mobile payment in ways that only China's unique situation allows. However, these benefits come at a cost: while these aspects enabled China's mobile payment revolution, they hinder its global expansion.

Historical: The Two

The first great leap occurred when China skipped the desktop era and went straight to mobile. Before desktops could proliferate across China, smartphones became popular.

In 2006, China was late to the game. The US already had 69% of the population online, where China had 10%. Desktop computers were they only means of getting online, and they were too expensive and bulky for the Chinese market - China had a lower average income and smaller living spaces. Even China's small 10% is somewhat skewed as many did not own personal computers but instead were more likely to access the internet via communal desktop computers at cyber cafés or public libraries. Where the US quickly embraced desktop computers, China dragged their feet. (World Bank, 2022)

This changed in 2007 with the release of the iPhone. When smartphones arrived in China, the low price, mobility, and convenience gave people the first viable means of consistently accessing the internet. China's internet users began to skyrocket. By 2009, internet users had tripled. Being late to connect to the internet ended up having major payoffs for China. They have been able to largely skip the era of personal computers. Without that baggage, China has been able to better embrace the mobile era. This helped China develop one of the most robust mobile internet ecosystems, with stand-out achievements in mobile payments. (World Bank, 2022; CNNIC, 2022)

China's second leap was avoiding dependency on credit and debit cards. Credit cards were never popular in China because the mobile payment phenomenon and the success of Alipay and

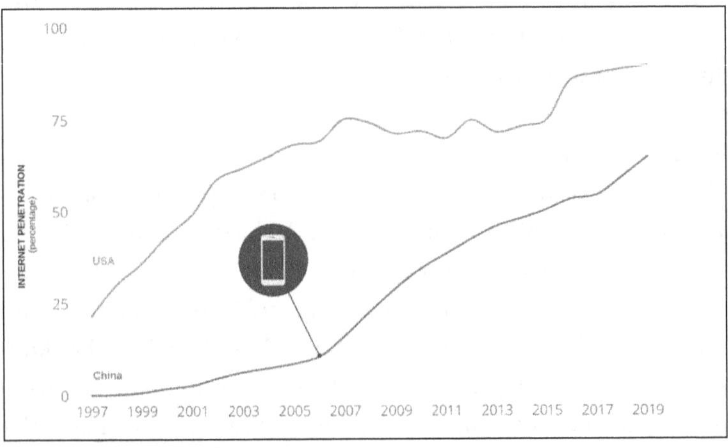

Figure 13: Internet Penetration in China and the USA.

China's internet uptake increases dramatically with the release of the smartphone. (World Bank, 2022)

WeChat Pay made them practically obsolete before they could gain serious traction. By contrast, credit and debit cards are well-established in Western countries, which inhibits consumers' willingness to adopt new forms of payment, such as mobile payment.

The US has been in love with credit cards for decades. Credit cards were first introduced in the 1950s, and debit cards in the 1970s. Americans cannot seem to drop them. In the US, for example, debit and credit cards are still the preferred payment method and continue to grow in popularity. According to the San Francisco Federal Reserve, 2017 marked the first-year American consumers used debit cards for purchases between $10-$24.99 at a higher rate than cash. (Kumar, Maktabi, & O'Brien, 2018) It seems inevitable that cash is no longer the preferred payment method in either China or the US. However, mature yet arguably antiquated forms of payment are holding back the West. At the same time, China charges headlong into a mobile payment future.

Cultural: Convenience is King

Chinese care more about convenience than privacy and security. Dr. Zhang Weining, an associate professor at Cheung Kong Graduate School of Business, one of China's top business schools, commented on this. In China, "all the young people are very busy chasing their dreams, and the old people don't care. That means privacy is not a top priority in people's lives." (Jacobs, 2018)

Chinese are accustomed to sharing personal information with others and are eager for the benefits of convenient digital solutions. This contributed to Chinese being more willing than people in many other countries to bind their bank cards to mobile payment platforms. Americans and other Westerners are more reserved in linking their financials to new online platforms.

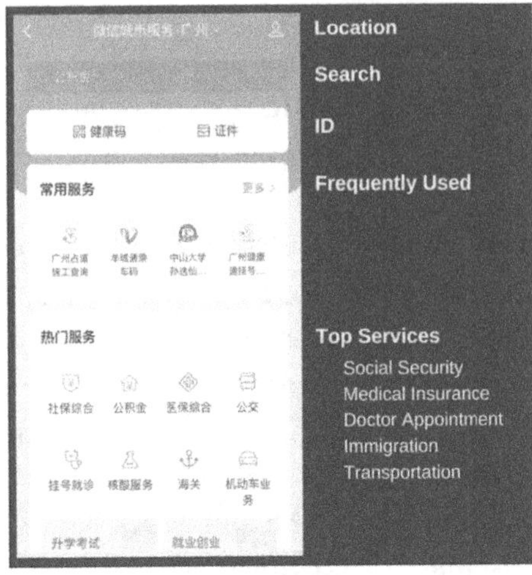

Figure 14: WeChat Public Services.

The feature brings government-operated services to the masses.

That said, recent history suggests that Chinese consumers are increasingly concerned about privacy as well. How this impacts the fintech industry remains to be seen.

Government: Centralized Incentives

China's government has been very impactful in China's digital revolution and the mobile payment phenomenon. Through the Central Bank of China, the CCP has been supportive of mobile payment. Implementing any new payment systems requires government support. Furthermore, through public (government)/private collaborations, such as Internet+, the Chinese government has furthered China's mobile payment adoption by incorporating China's extensive government services. On WeChat, this feature is called Public Services. Chinese people book hospital appointments, manage their medical records, pay traffic fines, register a marriage, and more. In 2019, people accessed government services via this WeChat function 660 million times.

To emulate this in a Western country, such as the US, would be difficult. For example, China has a centralized government where national powers exceed local and provincial levels of control. By contrast, the United States, emphasizing state's rights vs. federal authority, is decentralized with more than 50 states and territories having widely varying financial and legal systems.

Businesses: A Story of Two Giants

Four aspects of China's business environment fueled the growth of mobile payment systems: competitive incentives, a centralized landscape, a focus on cultivating user trust, and strategic vertical coverage of payment scenarios.

Competitive Incentives

China's digital revolution has been marked by fierce competition. As previously described, China's popular ride-share platform acquired deep capital and fought fiercely with Uber. As the two competed, they offered monetary incentives for users and drivers, significantly increasing the adoption rate. This, in turn, increased the adoption rate of both WeChat Pay and Alipay.

The car rideshare struggle was just one battle of a decade-long war for mobile payment dominance between WeChat Pay (Tencent) and Alipay (Alibaba). The war rages on with continuous subsidies and incentives from red-packet kickbacks on small store purchases to coupons for ecommerce to rebates on bike-sharing apps. The two giants burned money in subsidies, invested in new payment scenarios, and created large-scale shopping promotions. For example, Single's Day, a sort of anti-Valentine's Day popularized by Alibaba, became the world's largest offline and online shopping day in 2018. (Shankar, 2018) The two players have often made headlines in China, increasing user adoption and educating China's masses. This healthy competition has been the fuel driving China's mobile payment phenomenon.

Centralized Landscape

Despite the immense opportunity, China's mobile payment landscape has become surprisingly centralized around only two players, WeChat and Alipay. On their own, each player can cover virtually all scenarios. They can be used online and offline, at the check-out counter in stores, and online for P2P transactions. Mobile payment tools are being used to buy huge assets, including homes and cars, and cheap food on the street. Mobile payment has virtually replaced petty cash. The payment scenarios used by the two platforms are endless and continuously expanding as the battle rages on.

The US, by contrast, has hundreds of apps, each of which covers only a few transaction scenarios: Facebook to share experiences, WhatsApp/SnapChat/Messenger to chat, Amazon

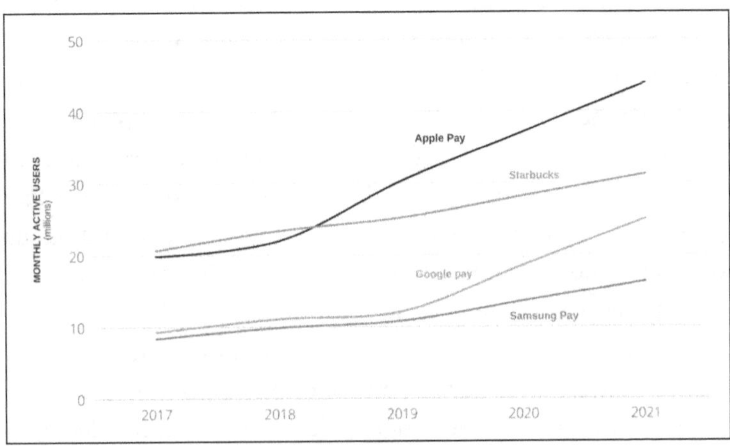

Figure 15: Mobile Payment Users in the US by Platform.

Only Apple Pay has overtaken Starbucks. (eMarketer, 2022; 2020 data estimated by author)

to shop online, PayPal to pay friends, Uber/Lyft to hail a car, and so on. By comparison, China only has two Superapps, WeChat and Alipay, that do virtually everything by connecting users with the greater Tencent and Alibaba ecosystems of goods and services.

Digital payment is a similar story. For Point-of-Sale (POS) mobile payments, Americans use multiple apps, such as Apple Pay and Google Pay. However, Apple Pay only overtook Starbucks' app at the end of 2019. Because their adoption rates have been so low, retailers like Starbucks and Wal-Mart have introduced their own POS payment apps, which have been surprisingly successful. This has made the POS payment market even more decentralized.

In P2P transactions, Americans most commonly use cash, but online they might use PayPal or Venmo. In ecommerce, Americans commonly use credit cards, while the tech-savvy use PayPal. Amazon Pay continues to struggle to find its niche. Lastly, online finance is dominated by individual institution-specific platforms, such as TD Ameritrade, an American online stock trading platform half a century old.

In regards to user convenience, having multiple payment platforms is like having multiple currencies. Imagine having twenty different currencies for a country - it would be a mess. Many currencies would quickly become useless. It would be difficult to manage or to know in which currency to pay, and so on. This is in large part why the majority of European countries adopted a single currency, the Euro. This is an existing challenge in the US mobile payment landscape. Do I pay you using Snapcash, Apple Pay, Venmo, PayPal, Amazon Pay or one of the many other payment products?

China's digital payment experience is vastly different, as it is dominated by just two players, WeChat Pay and Alipay. Within both of these, a user can pay at POS, send money to a

	Pay People	Pay Business
Online	Red Packet Virtual QR Code Money Transfer	Official Account 3rd Party Payment Mini Program
Offline	**Scan QR Code** Payer scans the Payees QR code, reviews amount, and confirms payment.	**Be Scanned** Cashier scans payer's phone with POS scanner. Payment automatically initiated.

WeChat User

Figure 16: Ways to Pay.

The many different ways to pay on WeChat.

friend (P2P), pay online (ecommerce), get a micro-loan, and manage finances. This dramatically reduces barriers to entry for both users and merchants and has accelerated China's mobile payment revolution.

Not only is China's digital payment more centralized, but it also offers multiple ways to pay, which again lowers barriers. For example, users can pay online and send red packets to one another or pay offline, scanning each other's QR codes. In addition, users can scan the QR codes of businesses or have the business scan a user's QR codes to request payment. This multi-pronged approach, outlined in the mobile payment segment of the WeChat Story, enables all types of businesses and organizations to enter the mobile payment arena, creating a continuous user experience.

User Trust

Lastly, and the most subtle, is the continuous focus on cultivating user trust. Both Tencent and Alibaba have increasingly focused on creating value for users and generating goodwill and confidence in their platforms. Alibaba has accomplished this through practical means by offering everything conveniently and cheaply in ecommerce. On the other hand, Tencent has maintained user value creation as its highest priority. Most notably, Allen Zhang created an entire product philosophy based around user value creation for WeChat which he shares with the public in his annual WeChat conference seminars. These strategies have given Chinese users sufficient peace of mind to opt-in by linking their bank cards to their accounts.

Vertical Coverage of Payment Scenarios

Both WeChat and Alipay have ensured that mobile payment in China becomes ubiquitous by focusing management on key vertical markets. This is designed to provide high rates of adoption in multiple business scenarios and across the economy. Payment scenarios traditionally cash-based, such as the wet markets, where urban residents buy their daily food, are included. Still common across China, wet markets are timeless and not easily replaced by the less successful though more modern supermarkets. They have remained virtually unchanged for hundreds, maybe thousands, of years. Yet, wet markets became another battleground for mobile payments almost overnight, with QR codes listed at every stall. The same was true for taxis. In just a few months, most taxis suddenly had a personal QR code displayed for users to scan and pay with WeChat Pay or Alipay.

China's mobile payment players focused on scenarios one at a time, ensuring widespread penetration in each before moving on. First peer-to-peer, then taxis, next wet markets, and so on. This allowed users to know when they might need their wallet and when they could simply leave it at home. Thus, scenario by scenario, Chinese people gradually left their wallets at home for good.

18

THE FUTURE OF MOBILE PAYMENT

AS WE HAVE SEEN, a few key elements drove China's mobile payment phenomenon. First, China lagged behind the world in personal computer and bank card adoption. Rather than try to catch up, China skipped both eras and focused on smartphones and mobile payment. Second, with a history of reduced privacy, China had fewer concerns over privacy and security (compared to the West) and was eager to adopt mobile payment for economic benefits and convenience. This sentiment was furthered by the two tech giants' loud and exciting competition and facilitated by the focus on user value, which provided Chinese consumers with the peace of mind necessary to jump on the bandwagon. Third, China's centralized government and its support of the mobile payment era further eased progression as the tech giants thoroughly covered every scenario possible.

China is now reaching full saturation of mobile payment adoption for its smartphone users as their preferred way of transacting business. How will mobile payment continue to grow? What (or where) is the next frontier for China's mobile payment battle? Who is in a better position, WeChat or Alipay? What are the future challenges for mobile payment players?

Mobile payment is rapidly embracing new technologies in China and leveraging China's growing international influence to go global. WeChat Pay and Alipay, representing Tencent and Alibaba, will continue to brawl, with Tencent currently having some advantages in the social arena. Yet, China's influence will not be sufficient for the platforms to truly go global. It seems likely that international players, like Apple Pay or Google Pay, will slowly but surely win the global mobile payment market.

New Tech in China

China's tech scene has been testing and incorporating new technologies and systems into its mobile payment ecosystem. However, one consistent factor of China's digital revolution journey has been the successful application of existing technology. The QR code is the quintessential example. Invented in Japan and written-off in the West as the 1990s failed fad, QR codes were the basis of China's mobile payment phenomenon.

One of the latest technologies to hit the ground running in China is facial recognition payment. First popularized by Apple's 'Face ID,' facial recognition payment is expanding beyond the

Figure 17: Facial Recognition Payment.

A woman uses a checkout counter with Alipay facial recognition at a supermarket in China. (VCG Photo, 2019)

smartphone camera. For example, Chinese consumers can self-checkout at supermarkets; they pay by facing the facial scanning screen. Similarly, consumers can purchase items from vending machines. China is seeing extensive adoption of facial payment, which is forecast to continue and is predicted to reach 761 million users in 2022. (eMarketer, 2019)

Not all technology that addresses consumer payments has been successfully applied in China. For example, the ability to pay without cashiers led to a sudden boom in unmanned stores in China. These were small stores where consumers entered the shop and used only their smartphones to pay. They would scan a QR code on an item and purchase via their phone, no clerks, no staff, not even a check-out counter. The industry attracted US$620 million of funding in 2017 alone. However, the fad did not last long. By mid-2018, many of these stores began to close, causing major players, Alibaba and JD.com, to cancel plans for unmanned store expansion. (PYMNTS, 2019)

China Going Global

Chinese digital products have a history of struggling to expand internationally. An exception is ByteDance, the owner of TikTok, which has made internationalization and global coverage a strategic priority. Like Alibaba and Tencent, the mainstay tech giants have always had a China-first strategy with global expansion a distant secondary objective. However, the tech giants' China-first digital products are generating a growing interest in the China market. This has garnered newfound respect in the global arena. As a result, WeChat Pay and Alipay have become particularly popular in a few scenarios that bridge China to the rest of the world. As these scenarios grow in popularity, the world will begin to see the mobile payment battleground spread beyond China.

Cross-Border Payment

As China's economy has grown, wealthier and bolder Chinese people have become more interested in international travel and vacations. As a result, Chinese outbound tourism has been the fastest-growing primary tourism market for years. While in the grand scheme of China's mobile payments, outbound tourism is a small segment, WeChat Pay and Alipay are eager to claim as much of this payment pie as possible. Cross-border payment provides international exposure and is a stepping-stone for future global expansion. It also offers more news-making milestones to impress users, investors, and potential partners. Beginning with Hong Kong, Macau, and Taiwan, China's cross-border payment had expanded to cover roughly 50 countries and regions by 2019.

While China's massive scale makes numbers seem small compared to itself, these are relatively big numbers for other countries. For example, in 2018, Chinese tourists became Australia's top tourist group in three categories: 1) most visitors from one country, 2) highest total spend, and 3) greatest forecasted growth. Similar stories abound throughout the APAC region. As a result, tourism boards and private companies eager to cater to this tourist market have accelerated cross-border payment adoption of WeChat Pay and Alipay.

International Pay

China's mobile payment has expanded to users beyond mainland China, beginning in 2017 with Hong Kong. This allowed citizens of Hong Kong to register a WeChat Pay Hong Kong or Alipay HK account specific to Hong Kong. This enabled users to make purchases locally and share money P2P with Hong Kong dollars. The services were separate from the WeChat Pay or Alipay services of mainland China. This process was repeated again when WeChat Pay launched a digital wallet specific to Malaysia in 2018. As of 2022, WeChat Pay has only officially launched overseas wallets in these two regions. Alipay has launched its own brand or adopted the brand of an acquired local company in multiple overseas countries.

Inbound Tourism

Continuing to expand their user base to people outside mainland China, at the end of 2019, WeChat Pay and Alipay began allowing international visitors to utilize their payment services. The two payment tools allow visitors to link to their international bank cards, Visa, Mastercard, American Express, etc. In 2019, China received 145 million inbound tourists. This helps the two players to increase their exposure and utility to an international audience. (CGTN, 2020)

Historically, WeChat and Alipay (and their parent companies, Tencent and Alibaba) have struggled to expand internationally through their Chinese digital products. However, as China's significance has grown internationally, these China-focused platforms have gained increasing interest from the international community. Chinese outbound tourism is one factor; the Chinese are the largest and fastest growing tourist market for many countries. Another is the elusive and massive Chinese consumer market. WeChat and Alipay have been leveraging their China-dominance to slowly grow their global influence in a bid to become China's best Superapp. However, who will win this battle is still unclear.

Future of Mobile Payments: WeChat Pay vs. Alipay

Both WeChat Pay and Alipay have unique advantages. WeChat Pay's benefits derive from its social roots and the entire WeChat ecosystem. As previously discussed, Red Packets were the key to WeChat Pay's initial explosive adoption. WeChat dominates in scenarios that combine social interaction and payment features. WeChat is the Chinese go-to preferred platform for recommending products to friends, group-buying, sharing coupons, and other social-inspired payment activities. Lastly, the advent of mini programs sealed WeChat's position as an efficient, all-encompassing ecosystem.

Counterintuitively, WeChat Pay's advantages come from the ecosystem as a whole and from outside of its payment function. Highly functional and light mini programs, invented by WeChat and optimized for the platform, power efficient interactions between users and businesses. WeChat Pay's global expansion has been focused on partnerships with local payment partners who facilitate cross-border payment. This reflects WeChat Pay's growth within China, which has generally focused on smaller investments and partnerships.

Alipay's advantages derive directly from its payment functionality. Alipay was the first entry into the mobile payment market and predated WeChat Pay for several years. Chinese users' general sentiment is that Alipay is more secure and better for large payments. Alipay's "Sesame Credit" is Alibaba's own devised credit score system. It combines two of Alipay's strengths: the platform's financial focus and its more extended payment history. As users make purchases, they gradually raise their Sesame Credit. This provides them a wide range of benefits, such as waiving deposit fees for renting cars or borrowing bike-shares, or getting a better mortgage rate on purchasing a home.

Alipay's expansion has been focused on verticals in payment and tends towards heavy investments and acquisitions. Expanding globally in cross-border payment, Alipay purchases or invests in local players and owns the cross-border payment system. WeChat Pay, by contrast, partners with local players and lets partners manage most of the financial transaction process.

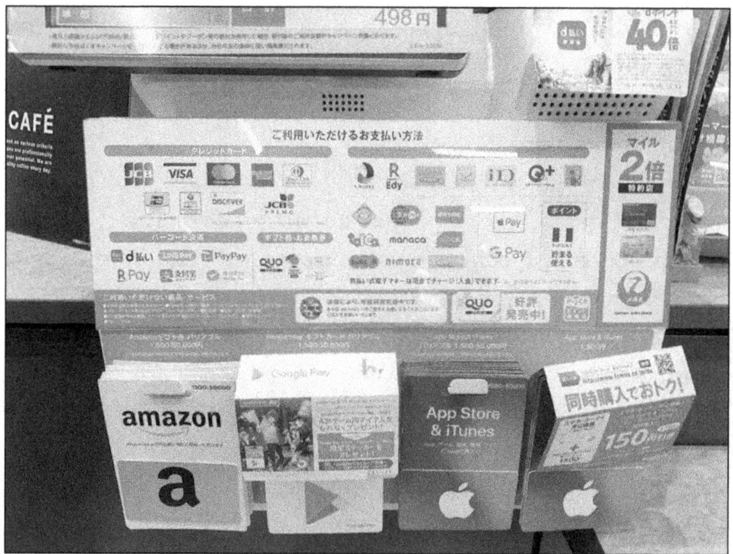

Figure 18: A Japanese 7/11 Supermarket Check-out.

A consumer is hit with a sea of payment tool logos when buying something at 7/11 in Osaka, Japan. Can you find Alipay and WeChat Pay?

Alipay seeks to control the financial strategy and focuses on its ecommerce roots and covering practical payment scenarios to generate more usage. At the same time, WeChat Pay looks for more nuanced techniques that might leverage mini programs or their social advantage.

Both China's major payment players find it challenging to differentiate on the international level. This is demonstrated by 7/11 convenience stores in Japan, where customers see a list of dozens of payment options. WeChat Pay and Alipay are lost in a sea of payment brand icons. With countless payment tools rising worldwide, WeChat Pay and Alipay will struggle to differentiate in the international arena. WeChat Pay and Alipay's rise to global prominence is primarily due to China's rise in the international market. The two players will continue to expand and grow by leveraging their roots as kings of the China market. However, this advantage is simultaneously their limitation. They will find it difficult to outgrow China and go global.

Future of Payment Worldwide

International expansion is where US companies will have an advantage in the long run. The same barriers that protect Chinese tech firms from global competition also prevent Chinese tech firms from expanding outside of China. As a result, the US and other countries with fewer barriers will be better positioned for international expansion.

China benefited from the early widespread adoption of smartphones and mobile payment systems. By 2019, 81% of China's smartphone users had made a mobile payment transaction, compared with 29% in the US that same year. (Cheung, 2019) This has given China's payment apps, WeChat Pay and Alipay, a big head start. However, other countries' adoption rates are gradually catching up. In recent years, Apple Pay has been steadily expanding globally, with an additional boost from COVID-19 fueling demand for contactless payment. In 2021, US Apple Pay had 44 million users in the United States and 507 million global users.

Apple Pay, PayPal, and Google Pay appear to be the strongest players in the international payment market. As mobile payment grows in importance, past strong players, such as Starbucks and Wal-Mart, and even Samsung, have significant limitations as payment tools. Starbucks and Wal-Mart do not have the capacity or the need to expand past their own retail payment scenarios. With a current estimate of 100 million payment users, Samsung Pay is not well-positioned strategically, as it is primarily a hardware manufacturer. Google Pay can address Samsung phones and many other android phones while also managing other scenarios from desktops and Google's array of connected services. PayPal has had consistent yet very marginal growth and seems to be outplayed by Apple Pay and Google Pay, which are better suited to take advantage of the smartphone era.

In the near term, Apple Pay has the strongest strategic position. Apple iOS users have always been more willing to spend money in the app store than Android users. This is due to several factors. Apple phones are more expensive, attracting a user base more willing to spend, and iOS's protected ecosystem cultivates more trust in the platform. Apple's product positioning is a more restrictive and controlling ecosystem, creating a gated community for its users. Users trade off the ability to customize and enjoy do-it-yourself capabilities for simplicity and greater overall security. 'Simple' and 'secure' are the two fundamental components users require to gain enough peace of mind to bind their bank cards. Apple's product positioning perfectly matches the demands of mobile payment.

However, in the long run, Apple Pay faces a similar limitation to Alipay and WeChat Pay. Apple Pay is restricted to its gated community, that is, users of the Apple operating system, just as Alipay and WeChat Pay are to a large extent limited to their Chinese users. While this will benefit initial growth for Apple users, in the long-term, the payment tool is doomed to not expand past the Apple user community. As of September 2021, Apple users are only a quarter of global smartphone users, while Google's Android makes up the majority of the remaining three quarters.

Google Pay has the right strategic mix for the long term, and Google has been making the right moves. In 2018, Google merged its array of payment tools (Google Checkout, Google Wallet, Android Pay, and Google Tez) into a single brand called "Google Pay." While 'Android' is specific to mobile phones and one operating system, 'Google' is agnostic. Google Pay is available on Android phones, iOS phones, web browsers, and many other forms. While the new brand will need time to cultivate user trust, Google Pay's association with the beloved Google search engine, popular on every device worldwide, should similarly pave the way for its adoption as a ubiquitous payment tool.

Lastly, Amazon Pay and Facebook's Libra are worth mentioning. The relationship between the two payment tools mirrors that of Alipay and WeChat Pay. A competition between the two would likely have similar results to China's mobile payment battle. Yet, smartphone operating system players were generally absent in China's mobile payment world, allowing Alipay's and WeChat Pays success. Amazon Pay is already late to the game, and Facebook's Libra has not been launched. Apple Pay and Google Pay will likely have strong footholds before either competing payment tool can properly launch.

Despite starting in China, it is clear that the payment-led digital revolution has moved beyond its borders. Similar to the likes of WeChat, we are now seeing major global players developing payment solutions alongside larger closed-loop systems. As a result, businesses see tremendous monetization opportunities in connecting social media, ecommerce, and services. The mobile payment represents the key linking element.

China, propelled by WeChat, is ahead of the world. Domestically, mobile payments proliferate at every level of interaction in Chinese society. However, the unique historical, cultural, government, and business factors that contributed to China's early mobile payment boom also limit its domestic companies from expanding overseas. Examining WeChat Pay and China as a case study is helpful for those wanting to glimpse the future of payment globally and those exploring the Chinese market.

Whatever comes next in payments, a Superapp strategy will

likely be a major element. How did WeChat become the world's first example of a Superapp? What even is a Superapp and how do we know what is a Superapp or just another app? What are Superapp's success factors? The answers are both intuitive and technical. Intuitive because an app is a user-centric cultural phenomenon, and technical because we need a fundamental standard definition which supersedes subjective experience.

Part 4

Superapps

Developed within China's unique internet, Superapps catalyzed China's digital growth. Their success within China has grown beyond China's borders. To better understand this, in Part 4, we expand and broaden our definition of a Superapp and the context and elements required to create a successful example. Then we explore real business cases in China to illustrate how global professionals might prepare for a Superapp future.

As we have seen, 'Superapp' was popularized to describe WeChat. By 2017, adoption was widespread, with an incredible number of people doing a vast array of things within a single application. Users were doing things within WeChat that previously required multiple distinct and unrelated applications to execute with a smartphone. A Superapp, such as WeChat, is a mobile phone app with which users can do so many things that it effectively becomes the operating system of their phone, and the center of their digital lifestyle.

As the smartphone and app market become more mature, studies have shown that people are decreasingly likely to download new applications of any type. A Superapp enables a user to engage new products and services using mini apps (the global-standard term for 'mini programs') and other tools within the Superapp, thus eliminating the need to acquire and download new technology. In China, Superapps have combined the low barrier-to-entry and simple transactions with a massive user community and powerful tools like payments and mini programs. This synergy enabled new business models within Superapp ecosystems, giving birth to innovations that return clear value to users and increase the visible worth of Superapps themselves.

As WeChat grew in popularity and functionality, other apps began emulating the Superapp strategy. Alipay followed closely behind, enabling broad services. WeChat and Alipay didn't individually go public, but the market value of each Superapp has been estimated above $100 billion USD. Others in China followed, including Meituan with a whopping $340 billion in 2021. Neighboring Southeast Asia is emulating this strategy with startups Grab and Gojek, valued at US$40 billion and US$10 billion respectively. On the App Store, Grab is called "Grab Superapp", defining itself as a superapp. This may be a form of self-determinism, or a strategy to encourage investor funding by using the buzzword to identify Grab more closely with successful Chinese Superapps.

Entrepreneurs worldwide want in on the action. Big companies are developing their own Superapps, many initiating Superapp projects and assembling independent agile teams focused on iterative, user-centric, innovative development to ensure that applications address user needs. Small startups announce the launch of new apps with enticing names, such as the "Superapp of the West," or the next "Superapp of India." All want to jump on the Superapp bandwagon. However, many fail to understand what a Superapp is and what developing one requires.

19

Defining 'Superapp'

Mike Lazaridis, the founder of Blackbery, coined the term, Superapp, in 2010, as an app that would offer "a seamless, integrated, contextualized and efficient experience." These would be "a new class of mobile applications that make you wonder how you ever lived without them." (Ponnappa, 2019) Sadly, the Lazaridis vision of the Superapp failed to materialize as the Blackberry empire crumbled due to security issues and increasing competition from Android and iOS operating environments. However, several years later, the 'Superapp' concept would be realized by developers half a world away who had likely never heard the term.

To the average person, a Superapp is one that does virtually everything a smartphone can do – effectively, it's the Swiss Army knife of apps. 'Superapp' was the term used to describe WeChat due to its incredible utility and popularity. Limitless products and services were available to buy and use on the app; dozens of tools, such as payment functionality and mini programs were available; and a billion users used the app throughout the day. Yet a more technical definition is required to analyze and better understand Superapps.

A Superapp is a mobile application that has achieved critical scale with respect to users and content, with tools enriching their interactions. Users come first and always remain the cornerstone of a Superapp. Content includes the products, services, and information offered by organizations, such as businesses, bloggers, government, etc. Tools enable efficient and dynamic interaction among content and users. Tools might include payment functionality that enables payment transactions and purchases, mini apps that facilitate complex interactions, or WeChat's Official Accounts or Facebook's Business Pages that create a standard format through which organizations engage users. Superapps achieve scale by leveraging a platform model.

A definition of critical scale is based on context, in that what suffices for one group may be insufficient for another. However, if there is sufficient content to address most aspects of a user's daily life, critical scale is achieved. Similarly, if there are sufficient tools to enable dynamic user interaction with content, and enough users to benefit and utilize them, the critical scale requirement has been met.

Today, Superapps achieve this critical scale by leveraging a platform and platform strategy. A platform enables interactions of entities, and then platform strategy maximizes the benefits of those interactions. By enabling valuable interactions, platforms attract

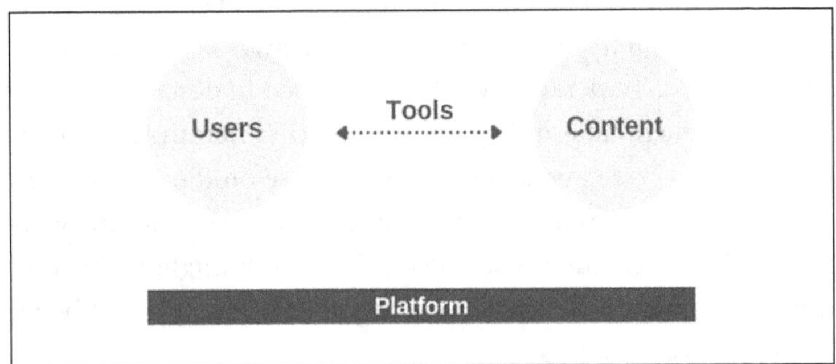

Figure 19: The Superapp model.

Users and business content interact on a platform.

more participants. Users attract businesses to make content, and content attracts users. Tools increase the value of the interactions and make the platform even more enticing. Superapps begin with users and then reach a tipping point where users attract more users and also content until reaching critical scale.

Users

Superapps are user-based with a focus on maximizing traffic. This is analogous to footfall in the age of brick-and-mortar retailers. The scale of users is measured in terms of *quantity*, which is the number of registered users, and *quality*, which is users love of the Superapp. Quality includes assessing how frequently users access the app, the time they spend on the app, and what they do on the app - which may include a financial component, i.e., what do they buy? - during each access period. A mixture of the two measurements - quantity and quality - has become a standard digital tech measure, the Monthly Active Users (MAU). Other quality measures might include those involving user content creation that enriches the value of the platform, such as how many photos or videos a user uploads and shares with others.

Implicit in this discussion is the understanding that not all users are equal. Some people will be much more frequent and loyal users than others. Still others might not use the app frequently, but have deep pockets and spend more money per use than more frequent users typically do. All user activities become factors in characterizing the quality of a user community.

WeChat's international expansion story emphasized the importance of quality users who love the product from the beginning. At one point, WeChat had 100 million registered users outside China. Unfortunately, most of those users no longer use the app, as they were 'zombie users', a term for individuals that frighten product creators. Zombie users create an account, do a few things, and for multiple reasons, abandon the account. A zombie user might be someone who accessed a chatting app and realized none of their friends were using the app; "*this is useless,*" they think, and close the app. When new users access the application, they see other users are inactive, which discourages them from continuing to use the application. They assume the platform is dead, drop it, and become new zombie users. In this way, zombie users create a cycle of death for fledgling platforms, in that the presence of zombie users encourages more users to become zombies. Furthermore, when a user stops using an app, a negative association with the app develops. It is very difficult to re-engage users after initial abandonment. While WeChat internationally had a large number of users, the quality of the users, as evidenced by their behavior on the site, was poor.

Theorectically, a Superapp can be manufactured without initial users. This would be analogous to building a city without people. Governments manufacture cities with the assumption that they will populate once the infrastructure is in place. While there are a few decently successful cases, eg. Brazilia and Canberra. Yet, this approach can fail when no on moves in, resulting in infamous ghost cities. Typically, cities, like most Superapps, are built in an iterative, gradual process that is integrally bound to the community that will inhabit the city.

While the cornerstone of a Superapp, an app needs more than users to become 'super'. Whatsapp is a good example of this. With roughly 2 billion active users, Whatsapp easily has the most users of any app in the world (Messenger comes a distant second with 1.3 billion). Whatsapp has users. However, Whatsapp lacks the content and tools that define a Superapp. To become a Superapp, Whatsapp would need to create a platform to attract businesses that cultivate content and create tools for users to dynamically engage with that content.

Content

What truly makes an app 'super' to users is the amazing number of things they can do with it. Content includes all the features of an app with which users can engage and/or consume. Content might be user-created blogs and short-videos, brand-created articles, merchant's ecommerce shop-fronts, developer's games, government services, and many other items. A Superapp's content has both breadth and depth, where breadth is the number of categories available, and depth is the variety of operations within each category, so that each user gets the best value possible from using the Superapp.

The Chinese app Meituan, for example, covers a wide variety of categories. Meituan includes food and grocery delivery; hotel booking; restaurant and bar reviews; movie tickets; group buying; booking local services, such as haircuts, dog walking, and cleaning; and much more. The Meituan content is primarily goods and services, but within that content, there is also depth, especially in the food delivery category. Meituan has more than two million registered restaurants. In China, any restaurant that delivers food can do so through Meituan. In 2020, Meituan facilitated more than two thirds of China's food deliveries, dominating the market. Not surprisingly, it's a big market. (Buchholz, 2021) China's food delivery market size was just over US$102 billion, dwarfing the US market of US$19 billion. (Textor, 2021)

An app can be lacking in either breadth or depth or even both. Imagine a hypothetical app 'LameTuan', which offers all the same services as Meituan. However, while LameTuan has breadth (coverage of categories), it lacks depth (penetration within those categories). A user opens LameTuan to order food and finds only a few restaurants, none of which are appealing. Hoping to get some benefit, the user then moves on to order movie tickets and discovers that of the 15 cinemas in the city, only one sells tickets through the app. This user would likely move on, switching to Meituan or another Superapp that has sufficient industry penetration to provide more satisfying services. LameTuan is a wannabe Superapp, in that it covers a lot of industries, but it doesn't have sufficient depth to satisfy users. Both breadth and depth are needed to make a fully-fledged, successful lifestyle Superapp.

Interaction Tools

Interaction tools are the technology that enables users to engage with content. Key examples of these in WeChat include a native payment tool (WeChat Pay), Official Accounts, mini programs, User ID, and data sharing. Not all these features are necessary to meet the Superapp definition, but some advanced methods by which individuals and organizations can easily and dynamically interact with each other are required.

Tools allow organizations and users to interact in dynamic ways. A payment tool allows purchasing not just from businesses, but from other people. Official Accounts or business pages allow businesses to easily access a platform and engage with users. Apps with User IDs allow users to easily log into and link with other apps and platforms. Other tools facilitate location sharing (for deliveries), phone numbers, or other personal information with businesses to enable more services.

Since WeChat was the world's first Superapp, one method of unraveling the term Superapp is to understand the moment that WeChat achieved that status. I argue that WeChat became a Superapp in late 2016 when the WeChat Pay tool reached relative maturity and became well-integrated with content on Official Accounts. At the time, 600 million users could purchase a myriad of goods and services from 10 million Official Accounts. A great mass of users could do and buy practically anything – they were enabled by the extensive content and tools. WeChat had become a Superapp.

The following year, in 2017, WeChat released mini programs, which essentially upgraded Official Accounts, providing organizations a more complex tool for user interaction. The advent of mini programs solidified WeChat's Superapp status, but it was an extension of existing functionality and not integral to the definition.

Others have argued that Superapps are defined by the existence of mini apps. Gojek, an Indonesian Superapp, defines a Superapp as, "apps within an umbrella app." (Ponnappa, 2019) While mini apps are great tools, I argue they are not necessary to create a Superapp. In fact, in the early life of a Superapp, mini apps might be too complex and result in raising the barrier for market entry. The development of mini apps requires significant development investment, which slows content cultivation. A better initial solution would be use of virtual store fronts or business pages. Later on, the complexity of these store fronts could be expanded as both users and businesses become familiar with the platform and demand more complexity. This is an iterative growth strategy common among platforms and Superapps, which is examined more closely in later chapters.

Platform Perspective

All of today's Superapps are platforms. A platform is a thing that facilitates the interaction of other things. With network effects and an ability to scale, a platform is the best method of cultivating a critical mass of users and content.

Today, the word 'platform' has colloquially come to be synonymous with 'website' or 'application'. You might hear someone say, *"I got this photo off such-and-such platform,"* referring to the app they downloaded it from. Yet, the business model definition focuses on what a platform accomplishes. A platform enables the interaction of things. Platform strategy maximizes the benefits those things receive from the interactions. (Merriam Webster, 2022)

Throughout history, platforms have brought people together. In ancient Greece, Academies were places where scholars could gather and benefit from each other by exchanging knowledge. Agoras were physical marketplaces where merchants sold their wares and buyers moved from stall to stall to make purchases. In the modern day, digital ecommerce platforms, such as Amazon, replicate the agoras of antiquity, enabling sellers to interact with buyers. Even credit cards are platforms as they work with merchants and consumers to facilitate financial transactions between them.

Platforms create networks. Platforms enable people and things to connect with one another which creates networks. The number of participants on a network can scale the number of connections exponentially, which helps make platforms and the networks they host so valuable. The quality of these network connections, or network effects, also helps the network grow and be valuable.

Network effects can be positive, negative or neutral. The telephone is an example of something with a positive network effect. The telephone is made useful by other people having a telephone. The usefulness of a telephone increases in relation to the number of people who also have one. This is a positive network effect. A sandwich has no network effect. A sandwich will be just as nourishing and satisfying whether others do or don't have sandwiches. Cars can have a negative network effect as too many cars on the road create congested road traffic. Traffic decreases utility of cars, which is why big cities need to have

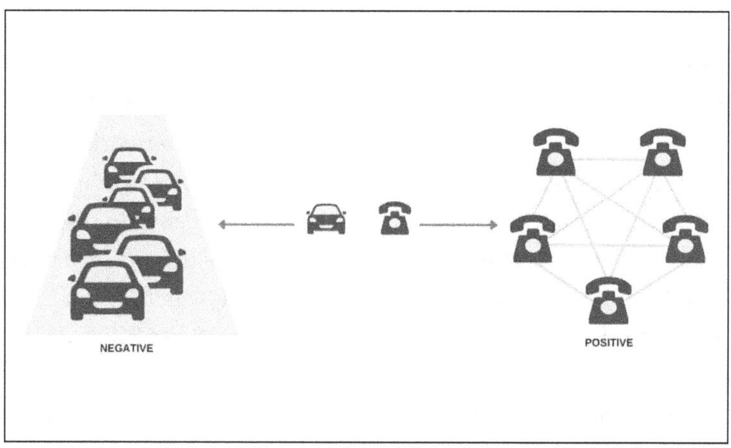

Figure 20: Positive and Negative Network Effects.

A phone has a positive network effect, it becomes more useful when more phones are present. A car has a negative network effect, it becomes less useful when more cars are present – the result is traffic.

mass transit such as subway systems. Although, my favorite example of a negative network effect is the fedora. Please, one per crew.

Platforms aim to optimize network effects. Intuitively, this means increasing positive network effects and minimizing negative. Telephones positive network effects were increased by the addition of a directly of phone numbers – this was the "Yellow Pages" in most places. This directory made it easy to find a person or organization's phone number which made telephones more useful. Returning to the example of car traffic, cities reduce this negative network effect with urban planning. They create larger roads and divert traffic around city centers where congestion is more likely, and they encourage and subsidize car-shares and public transport to reduce car travel to high demand areas.

An example of a digital platform optimizing network effects is Uber. Uber is another platform enabling the interaction of passengers and drivers. The positive network effects are clear. The more drivers the more benefit for passengers – a passenger can more quickly get a ride. The more passengers the better for drivers – a driver can more quickly get a passenger and continue to make money. Uber aims its entire app around most efficiently connecting these two parties to increase positive network effects.

Yet, there are negative network effects. Bad drivers can provide passengers with a bad experience. Uber aims to decrease these negative network effects. Passengers rate drivers on a scale of 1 to 5, if a driver has a rating of 4.6 or lower they can lose access to the service and/or be required to attend Uber driver training. (Shaban, 2019)

Platforms can snowball which is why they're effective means of cultivating scale. Yet, first a platform needs early participants. A platform needs to reach a tipping point by achieving a critical mass of participants. The tipping point is the number of users at which the benefits of positive network effects outweigh the costs of switching to the platform. At this point, the platform's user growth becomes self-perpetuating – users beget users. The

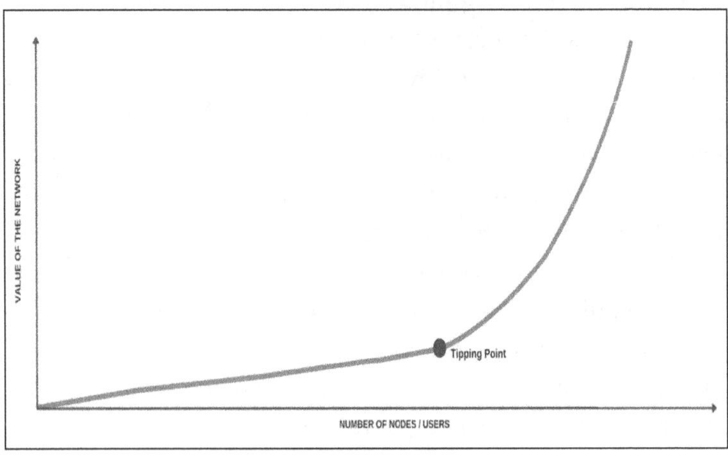

Figure 21: Tipping Point.

The tipping point is when the number of users make the network so valuable that new users start joining on. This is due to the positive network effects of the users.

platform quickly snowballs with exponential growth until it dominates the market.

The major challenge for most platforms is reaching that tipping point. This is often referred to as "the chicken and the egg program". How does Uber simultaneously get riders and drivers onto the platform? Or for a platform with only one group initially such as the telephone, how do you convince the first person to buy one?

Network effects can be a double-edged sword. Negative network effects can snowball to decrease platform users. Bad drivers provide passengers with bad experiences, this in turn causes the passengers to leave the platform. Less passengers makes the platform less attractive and less valuable to drivers. This then causes other drivers (even the good ones) to leave.

The platform model is currently the only means for a product to achieve critical scale, in both users and content, and become a Superapp. Hypothetically, if a single entity owns all products and services available to users, leveraging a platform to bring third-party products and services onboard is not required. For example, given that all businesses are state-owned, North Korea's ruling government (the Workers' Party of Korea) might create a full-service app without a platform. Another example, if Disney Theme Parks created an app that offered purchasing for all Disney goods and services, as well as, complex interactions within a Disneyland property, then this could be considered a Superapp within Disneyland's own little universe. Nevertheless, in neither the Disneyland or North Korea case could the product grow and go global, to become a true Superapp, without leveraging a platform model.

20

Superapp Success Factors

Leverage Platform Strategy

All of today's Superapps leverage platforms and platform strategy to reach critical scale. Platform strategy involves dissecting the groups on the platform, assessing their network effects and then optimizing them.

A platform can have one group or multiple groups. One group is called 'single-sided' while multiple groups is called 'multi-sided'. These groups have different connections. Same-side is connecting with others of the same group, while cross-side is one group participant connecting with another of a different group.

Dropbox, a file-sharing platform, is an example of a single-sided platform. It has only one group. Dropbox's core value is allowing people to save files and then share them with others. This creates same-side positive network effects. Users benefit from the presence of other users - the more people using Dropbox, the more people a user can easily share files with.

Single-sided platform has only one network effect, while a multi-sided platform with two groups has four network effects. Two same-side network effects - the two groups interacting with themselves - and two cross-side network effects - the two groups affecting each other. The cross-side network effect is two effects because it runs in both directions. Group A's effect on group B,

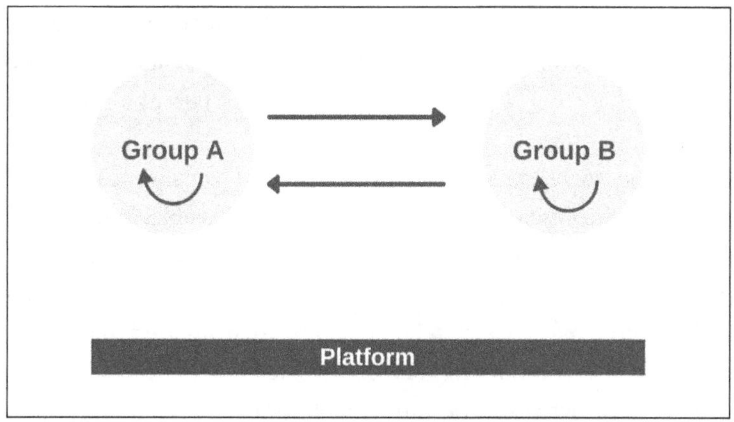

Figure 22: A Two-Sided Network Has Four Network Effects.

Two same-side; the effect of Group A members on other Group A members, and the same for Group B on itself. Two cross-side effects; the effect of Group A on Group B and the effect of Group B on Group A.

and group B's effect on group A.

The night club generalized in pop culture, is an example of a multi-sided platform with two groups, men and women, that have four network effects. The two same-side effects are men on men and women on women. Men have a negative same-side network effect, more men mean more competition, the term 'sausage fest' comes to mind. Women are slightly positive about the presence of other women; they feel safer in numbers. There are also two cross-side effects. The presence of men has a slightly positive network effect on women; women are attracted to men but many just go to dance and have fun. Lastly, the important one, women have a massively positive network effect on men. If a club is known for having a lot of women, men will pay virtually anything to get in. This is why clubs have "ladies' night" and let women in for free, while continuing to charge for men. More women will attract more men, yet the opposite isn't necessarily true.

Multi-sided platforms commonly begin as a single-sided

platform. They start with one group and later bring in more groups to become multi-sided. Other platforms start with two groups, like Uber with drivers and riders. Superapps start with one group; users.

In the early days, WeChat introduced several features to achieve critical scale of users as quickly as possible. While these features did not directly cause people to go download WeChat, they increased the utility of WeChat by increasing users same-side positive network effects. The features, examined in Chapter 11, all focused on making it easier for WeChat users to add other users. This increased the number of connections WeChat users would have with other users. The more connections, the more positive network effects, the more useful WeChat would be. The features increased positive network effects, and therein, the value of the platform which then attracted new users which would yet increase the value of the platform more.

Once the single group (users) is established, Superapps bring in other groups. After its growth phase WeChat brought businesses onto the platform with Official Accounts, explored in Chapter 12. Users had a positive cross-side network effect to businesses, for businesses the more users the better. With so many users, businesses quickly jumped onto the platform.

Yet, in the opposite direction, businesses can have a negative cross-side network effect on users. More businesses can mean more spam and ads. This means more businesses can be worse for users. Just think about a product you've used and enjoyed until it hit over-commercialization. more spam or over-commercialization,

To minimize these negative cross-side network effects, WeChat enforced a multitude of restrictions on businesses. A few examples:

1. Limitations on external links in articles so that users

didn't need to go elsewhere to gain value
2. A limit of three ads a day in Moments per user.
3. Businesses limited to sending four messages to followers per month in order to reduce spam.

Now if only I could just as easily reduce my e-mail and SMS spam.

User-Focused

Acquiring and maintaining value to the user is the top priority for a successful Superapp. This means embracing a user-first strategy. Users know when they are prioritized and benefiting from generated value. This knowledge helps to cultivate user trust in the platform, which encourages users to opt-in to new tools as they are available, access increased functionality, and share their data to facilitate activities and processes that the app provides. Data sharing built on trust leads to confidence in the app and convenience for the user, which, in turn, fosters goodwill toward the platform. Confidence in the platform extends to the goods and services accessed through the platform by implying that a trustworthy platform offers reliable products and services. This circular reinforcement ensures that the platform, the Superapp will continue to flourish and expand its user base.

High Frequency

In addition to user focus, user traffic is critical for a Superapp's success. Successful Superapps focus on building a following through a high frequency access scenario as a value proposition. This becomes the primary driver of user traffic, pumping life into the Superapp. The Superapp business model is to then redirect flow of user traffic into other areas to monetize.

I like to think of user traffic as a river. A successful Superapp's user traffic is the flow of a torrential river. Great content and services dig a deep riverbed and attract more water (users). The bigger the river, the better. The Superapp strategy is to then redirect water (users) to crops (monetizing services, e.g., insurance, ecommerce, ads, etc.). In this metaphor, the Superapp business model is about good irrigation and fertile fields. The Superapp cultivates a great river of user traffic and then efficiently guides the water to where it will produce the highest yield.

To attract a strong and constant flow of user traffic, a Superapp's core value proposition should be a high frequency need. The Superapp should be built around something that people will use continuously. Though frequency is the key factor, volume - a large number of people - also contributes to the value proposition. To discover what makes a great Superapp, Superapp designers should consider what people do all the time.

Communication is a high frequency activity practiced by virtually everyone in some form. Apps in the messaging, social media, micro-blogging, and other communication media are all great candidates for Superapps. Apps in this area include WeChat, Messenger, Snapchat, Whatsapp, Facebook, Twitter, etc. All of these apps have strong user bases and therein the potential to become 'super'. Yet, while Snapchat has added payments, Facebook and Twitter have brought on businesses, only WeChat has the content, tools and ubiquity necessary to achieve Superapp status.

Shopping is another activity people do all the time. They shop for groceries, household items, clothing, pet food, and other daily needs. Apps that support this are Alipay, JingDong, Meituan, and Amazon. Alipay and Meituan moved quickly to Superapp-ism, while Amazon continues to focus solely on ecommerce.

Transportation is another excellent candidate for a Superapp.

Most people travel every day and are willing to pay good money to do so with minimal anxiety. The frequency of this need is high, as evidenced by Uber, Lyft, Didi, Grab, Gojek, and others. Many of these ride-hailing and car-sharing apps are moving towards a Superapp strategy.

A specific transportation need, bike-sharing, became a frenzy of activity among startups in China. Massive investments were made, and billions in marketing and operations were spent. The craze occurred because of the high-frequency need for hyper-local transportation. Generally, people only need to take a cab once or twice a day; at lower socioeconomic levels, a taxi may be required no more than once or twice a month. However, hyper-local travel, traveling to destinations within 5 to 30 minutes of walking distance, is a constant need in China's urban areas. Chinese people walk 20 minutes to the nearest subway station or walk 15 minutes to their favorite restaurant for lunch. Using bike-share people could simply jump on a bike and get there in a quarter of the time. In major cities where people use public transportation, hyper-local transportation services are more likely be used than ride-hailing apps, e.g., Uber or Didi. Whichever bike-share platform emerged the winner would be an excellent candidate for becoming a new Superapp, or could channel a strong flow of traffic to an existing Superapp player.

What about a need that only applies to a specific group of people? For example, acquiring and using make-up are constant needs for many women. However, men generally do not use make-up. One could expect an app that aids in the application of make-up to be used primarily by women, which would limit the number of users. But if the app had all the women in America using it every day or several times a day, the app could cash-in on that traffic using a dynamic Superapp strategy.

Superapp candidates can be identified by examining the

same things that we have discussed throughout this book, which are those things that characterize and provide context to a population, and the degree and frequency of need or desire for goods or services. Once identified, the strategy employed by WeChat provides a blueprint for further exploration.

Positioning

Positioning is similar to branding and describes where a product or platform resides in the minds of consumers. It is the general impression that you have about a thing. People might think one app is great for buying luxury shoes, while another app is great for buying cheap electronics. For example, we have a clear notion about McDonalds' positioning; it provides fast, low-cost, reliably standardized food, while Apple's positioning references sleek, simple, high-quality electronics.

Positioning should begin as simple, minimalist, and clear: a fun chatting app; a practical ride-hailing app; a tech-savvy, product-reviewing app, etc. Each new element or feature added to the app should be carefully considered with respect to how it will influence positioning. New elements should be either within the Superapp's original market position or closely related. For this reason, Superapps are not built in a day, but are iterative in their development.

For example, WeChat's core value proposition is a messaging platform. This platform is completely C2C, users benefiting from the presence of other users. In the beginning, WeChat focused solely on growing user numbers and connections between users. The first dozen WeChat features were all focused on virality, which is the process of helping users add other users or invite others to use WeChat. As previously discussed, features that provided WeChat positioning included Shake-Shake; Message in a Bottle; QR codes and scan QR codes; Friend Radar; adding people from groups or Forward Contact; and invitation links. This early version of WeChat was solely a tool to add friends and communicate with friends. Initially, development focused on ensuring not only that new people acquired and used the app, but that they connected with other people on the platform as quickly as possible.

When WeChat incorporated its first new category of functionality, Moments, which was a Social Networking System (SNS) that enabled users to broadcast to other users, its positioning evolved to reflect this new feature. At this point, WeChat had not incorporated businesses, payment tools, or operating systems within the app. It continued to be very focused on the single function of users communicating with other users. However, after this segment was well addressed, WeChat added new user options in the form of businesses and bloggers. Even then, these were introduced to the app via Official Accounts, which forced these entities to communicate with users via messages in the same way that other app features were used. This expanded the user community and enhanced the value of WeChat while retaining its core value proposition as a messaging platform. It kept its positioning as new elements were introduced to the app.

Iterative

As we have seen, Superapps start as simple applications and grow step-by-step into 'super' status. This is a primary challenge in developing a Superapp as a new product. A better method is to begin with a well-designed basic application with an established user base and clear position. By leveraging platform strategy and a strong user following, the app will grow into a Superapp.

As Superapps expand and bring businesses onto their platform, they should focus on either a single or a very few well-chosen industry verticals. This is critical because depth is as important as breadth in considering industry content that will grow your base and enhance your position. As in the previous 'zombie user' story, if a user goes to buy shoes in a rising Superapp's ecommerce shoe category, but finds that his favorite shoes aren't available and there are only three other brands from which to choose, the industry vertical does not have the depth to enhance the Superapp. This leaves the user with a negative association regarding purchasing on the app, which results in a zombie user. A strong development strategy focuses on identifying limited industry verticals with significant followings, deep product offerings, and positive branding to amass a plentitude of content and ensure an expanding user base.

Similarly, in identifying and courting the ideal user, a step-by-step approach should be utilized by focusing on one core demographic and then, once satisfactorily saturated, extending to periphery demographics. For example, first focusing on young male gamers, then females, add non-gamers, and ultimately users of all-ages.

Architecture – Lowering barriers to entry

A well-architected Superapp platform lowers the barrier of entry for users and businesses, and facilitates development by enabling users to easily access functionality. Architecture refers to the technical infrastructure of the Superapp and how different parties onboard or connect with it.

The scale of both users and content is the most important aspect of a Superapp. In the beginning of platform development, it's a race to build scale rapidly. This is especially important in addressing the chicken-and-egg conundrum of platforms. If people go on the platform and see a limited user community or no content, they leave the platform and don't return. If businesses go on the platform and find no users, they too will leave, which in turn leads to no content and fewer users.

To build scale, fledgling Superapps should make barriers to entry as low as possible. Take Twitter as an example: The platform has a cap on how many words a person can share, which helps influencers to avoid oversharing or overthinking their content before posting. This simple rule lowers the barrier-to-entry for creating content. Simultaneously, the rule lowers the barrier for reading content, since everything is short.

A mistake fledgling Superapp developers make today is jumping straight to creating a lite-OS on their app. This forces businesses to develop mini apps in order to on-board and create content. What if you had to develop a mini app to post a tweet on twitter? There'd be very few content creators. For fledgling Superapps with a small user-base, this is too high a cost for businesses - it raises the barrier-to-entry too high. Instead, fledgling Superapps should identify and use minimalist strategies. How can I bring on businesses to offer their goods and services in the easiest way possible? What is the bare minimum they need to offer content?

WeChat, for example, began by offering businesses Official Accounts. An individual could set one up in seconds, while could be up and running in minutes. The two-tiered approach meant 'individuals' could register with an ID card and didn't require a business license. Once set up, Official Accounts had a simple and standardized platform to send articles and interact with users. The feature was an instant success. Just two years after launching Official Accounts, WeChat had 8 million Official Accounts. These Accounts created an abundance of content, which attracted still more users. If WeChat had begun with mini programs, businesses would have been reluctant to invest the resources to on-board; less content would have been created, and fewer users would have joined WeChat.

User Design

Similar to the criticality of architecting an app with excellent infrastructure, good user design ensures a lower barrier to entry for new users. The success or failure of user design begins with the first exposure to the app, which comes when a new app is needed to accomplish a task. A user should not be required to search for it and read directions in order to download and install. The app should be easy to find and make operational. Many modern-day apps succeed by implementing a user design that enables a user to follow a few self-evident steps quickly and easily to download the app and register the account. Since the goal is to onboard users and have them using the application as quickly as possible, this feature is essential.

For most users, the first few minutes on an application are the most critical. A poorly designed application might request a plethora of information and permissions up-front. For example, you open the "Phromo" application and discover that Phromo needs to access your camera, your microphone, your ID credentials, and track your location in order to function. If you are like most users, requests for these permissions up-front will make you more cautious and, assuming you proceed, take additional time and effort before you can use the app. This raises the barrier-to-entry for many new users, because they become annoyed and confused by the installation process. At this point, users may decline to provide the information and reject the app completely. On the other hand, a good app helps a new user register quickly, allows her to accomplish what she came to do, and leaves her satisfied with performance and ready to return to the app in the future.

Permissions should only be required when they are relevant to a task a user wants to complete. For example, if you want to share a photo with a friend on Messenger, a pop-up should appear with a message: 'Do you want to give Messenger permission to access your Photos?' Permission requests should relate directly to what the user wants to accomplish.

Great product design is a core success factor of Superapps. Great design helps users enjoy their experience on the app and ensures they keep coming back, which increases user traffic and user loyalty to the Superapp, which are the main objectives of a Superapp. Product design is not specific to Superapps and other software applications. Ideally, it's in everything that humans create. Don Norman explains in his book, *The Design of Everyday Things* - the holy bible of the design world - that "design is concerned with how things work, how they are controlled, and the nature of the interaction between people and technology." Design in the software world is what people see when they open an app and how they interact with it. It is also the functionality the app offers and how well it performs. Design ranges from the aesthetics and general appearance to how the app is organized and the features it provides. Design is fundamental to all parts of creating a product because ensuring that the user interacts with the application is the end-goal of functionality. This is especially true for a Superapp.

To become a Superapp, the design has to be super. As with other aspects, a successful design strategy is iterative. Good apps begin simply and become more complex over time. This allows users to experience the journey, gradually learning an increasingly complex product.

Governance

Good platforms have good governance. Governance are the restrictions and incentives in place to encourage positive interactions between all parties. Interaction among parties enables platforms to generate value. The better the interactions, the more value generated. Good governance is important to ensure that interactions are the best they can be, and most importantly, that they are not bad.

Revisiting the earlier example of Uber, the platform encourages drivers to provide the best experience to riders by providing a review system. Uber drivers with high average reviews receive bonuses. Drivers offering a bottle of water or a mint to passengers became an industry standard, something unheard of in the era of taxis.

Smart Monetization

Superapps take the main flow of user traffic and divert it to money-making enterprises. Value Added Service (VAS) is about diverting user flow to profitable enterprises that benefit the user and the company. Conventional apps simply use ads. Ads divert user traffic to make money. However, there are some distinct differences between ads and VAS.

Ads direct users to a new place, leaving the app-controlled ecosystem. The result could be either positive or negative, but the impression left with the user will be associated with the original app. For example, an app could lead to a website to buy a shirt from a favorite band, but it might also turn out to be a scam, selling poor quality shirts that are obviously not signed by original band members. While the platform can place rules restricting where ads can lead and police organizations posting ads, control is limited and quality is difficult to maintain. The organizations posting ads might not have users' best interests at heart. Many of them are in it for a quick buck – how can they make money as quickly as possible? If ads on a platform lead to unsavory situations, trust in the platform will begin to decline. When trust declines, ads become less effective because wary users avoid them.

The VAS strategy diverts traffic from the Superapp's main functions but keeps it within the ecosystem. Users are diverted to products and services that are vetted by the Superapp, ensuring users receive the best experience possible. The Superapp benefits because it either receives a percentage of each transaction or the parent company is an investor in the product or service. For example, a user wanting to buy a shirt of their favorite band uses the ecommerce portal within a Superapp. This leads him to an ecommerce platform affiliated with the Superapp. When a shirt of poor quality with band signatures that are obviously fake is received, complaint to the ecommerce platform results in managing the situation to compensate the user. Furthermore, because everything is within a single ecosystem, the Superapp and the ecommerce platform ensure that the transition is incredibly smooth and the user experience excellent. This makes users happy and cultivates more trust in the Superapp and affiliated services, which increases the number of users and transactions.

Most Superapps start with a commercial use-case, which is a solution that fulfills a user need and involves a third-party. For Amazon, this was buying books. For WeChat, this was reading articles from the media, bloggers, and companies. In terms of platform strategy, the goal is to expand by introducing a new group or side. This should have a positive impact on users, expanding the range of functionality and usefulness of the Superapp.

21

THE GOOD AND THE BAD OF SUPERAPPS

SUPERAPPS HAVE become the latest trend with hundreds of companies and organizations worldwide simultaneously working on emulating the accomplishments of WeChat and other Chinese Superapps. The benefits of Superapps become obvious in the ludicrous market values that they achieve, which are based on assumptions of market share expansion, monetization, increasing user traffic, and so on. To better understand the sky-high hype around Superapps, it is useful to examine the many benefits of Superapps, as well as the associated costs and challenges. While some advantages are common to all digital platforms, others relate specifically to a Superapp strategy.

Benefits

First and foremost, Superapps provide tremendous user traffic. This is, in part, the core of the Superapp strategy. As a Superapp developer, your goal is to amass a large user base and excellent user traffic and then reroute that traffic into monetization ventures, such as food delivery services, ride-share, and games, or alternatively, follow the most direct path and market ads to your increasing user traffic.

Superapps are expandable, extensible, and malleable because their components comprise a platform. They can extend into new fields, penetrating a fresh market to expand the products and services offered to users. This enables Superapps to grow iteratively and significantly as they encompass virtually all consumer-facing verticals. It also enables each module to expand without impacting other Superapp components.

Successful Superapps have a low barrier-to-entry. Users can access and begin applying a Superapp to access the wide-range of services available. Modern smartphone apps are focused on user-friendliness - generally more intuitive and easily accessible than desktop programs or their offline counter-parts. Superapps capitalize on the ease of use of single apps while providing a range of services through a common interface with consistent design.

Superapps have competitive durability. Same-side positive network effects mean that the more users engage with the Superapp, the more valuable it becomes. Similarly, cross-side positive network effects facilitate more businesses and content on the platform, attracting more users in an ever-expanding universe. Furthermore, Superapps have lock-in characteristics, which are features that dissuade users from switching to competing products. Factors that create lock-in include invested time, resources, and familiarity with the app, as well as potentially having user-created, non-transferable content on the platform.

Superapps enable businesses to engage people in their own digital space. Direct-to-consumer is a new trend in which brand retail and other businesses work directly with consumers, bypassing ecommerce platforms to directly engage users. Applications such as Shopify and Squarespace allow small businesses to create and manage their own ecommerce websites. Superapps provide an in-between option to large ecommerce sites. This middle ground allows individual brands to directly engage a user in their personalized digital space and maintain more direct control of the marketing channel.

Similar to Google, Apple ID, and Facebook, Superapps also provide login access to other digital platforms. This is both more convenient and secure in that it enables users to store and access their personal and private information in a trusted environment.

Superapps generate reams of data. The Superapp provides a digital space where lifestyle is created, reflected, and continuously expanded. Chatting with friends and discovering, purchasing, reviewing, and referring products, which are everyday user activities, produces an unprecedented quantity of granular data. Data can be analyzed to provide highly targeted and efficient ads or recommend better services to people, which further increases user value. Successful Superapps make data available to businesses and developers, which allows them to monitor user interactivity with their content, and improve their products or services in response to user perception. This enables them to better understand and engage with users, creating more value for businesses and the user community while increasing the value of the Superapp platform. As valuable as these data are, increasing government policy and regulation to protect user privacy and limit how intrusive marketing can become are impacting how data may be collected, utilized, and retained. Despite these changes, there are still vast amounts of new information to derive from deidentified data collected through user engagement with a Superapp.

Like any new technological innovation, Superapps have enabled new business solutions that create new user value. Consider the number of new product offerings that have resulted from the evolution of smartphones. The mobility, connectivity, and ease-of-use of smartphones has been the hallmark of the modern era, making possible entire new services like ride-sharing (Uber, Lyft), group-buying (Groupon), Pokémon Go, and geocaching games. Smartphones also improved and popularized mobility solutions based on geo-location, such as navigation (Google Maps) for driving, e-ticketing, live social media like Twitter or TikTok, and most recently, checking-in to locations via a QR code scan during the COVID pandemic.

The advent of Superapps, which have their genesis in smartphone technology, has enabled new business solutions. A billion people easily purchasing from a single platform with pre-loaded user information makes new business solutions. In China, this has seen business models take-off that are virtually unseen in the West. Examples include mobile electronic battery rental stations, smart karaoke boxes, smart 'relax rooms', and scan-to-pay vending machines. These solutions have ignited social ecommerce, creating, for example, Pinduoduo, which is now a $74 bn USD company. (Pinduoduo Inc., 2021)

Superapps have unprecedented market potential compared to traditional business models. As digital platforms, Superapps can scale with minimal investment. They are not constrained by geographic barriers. Therefore, the market potential is the entire world rather than one region or nation. Superapps typically offer each user a range of customization, which ensures both an excellent user experience and a sense of user ownership. Superapps also lend themselves to a variety of monetization strategies, which enables developers to test and deploy various models to determine the best strategy for both the platform and the user community.

Digital platforms are easily and inexpensively scaled. For this reason, Superapps can acquire high margins by targeting niche and long-tail markets that might not have appealed to more traditional generalized solutions.

Superapps facilitate a dispersion of innovation. Rather than depending on company employees to create new functionality or content, a platform model permits innovation from key players, including users, businesses, developers, and the government. At WeChat, people commonly said, "users will always be more creative than you." Considering this, instead of trying to create the best thing possible for users, WeChat offered users the tools to create new features. On my marketing team, this might simply mean hosting a marketing competition such as, "who can submit the best video that shows how they uniquely used WeChat during Chinese New Year?" Similarly, this mentality is put to use more fundamentally on a product level as Superapps enable platform players to create and share content.

Costs and Challenges

Superapps have many benefits, as evidenced by their high market value. However, the initial cost is significant, which explains why there are so few. This is typical of digital startups. However, the investment required to develop a Superapp exceeds the cost to develop a digital startup product. For one thing, Superapps need to delay monetization, which eliminates the potential for quick profits. Superapp development requires an initial focus on creating and marketing a user experience. This can render the platform unprofitable for many years and result in a much longer growth cycle than that required for most other platform types. Initially, Superapps must focus on driving user traffic, as wide acceptance and utilization are key to success. Any monetization that would inhibit this growth could be catastrophic.

Similar to the need to grow the user community, is the acquisition of an army of ecosystem partners. These are the businesses, influencers, developers, and other players who create the user content. Attracting each new group to the platform can require the investment of major time and resources.

Superapps require investment in top talent to ensure an

excellent user experience on then app, and, even then, the potential for failure is high. Talent of this caliber can be costly and difficult to hire and retain. Frequently, incentives other than financial, such as equity or a strong company vision are necessary.

This town ain't big enough for the two of us!

Superapps are designed to be all-encompassing. As such, it's difficult for multiple Superapps to coexist. Fierce competition and high upfront cost mean that there are very few successful contenders. Furthermore, since Superapps become so well entrenched and build competitive durability, it's difficult for new competition to enter the field. These factors limit the number of organizations willing to invest in and create a new Superapp. Largely due to this dominance and the depth of the relationship between the Superapp and individual users, Superapps are at risk from government and policy restrictions that tend to lead to limiting regulations. Superapps can dominate entire business arenas, which can lead other players and potential players to claim the Superapp has unfair advantages. This risks anti-trust allegations and government interference that can embroil the parent company in years of litigation.

22

Joining Superapps

Superapps, by definition, cover the broad scope of an industry vertical or activity. Currently, only a few exist. While there may be many Superapp projects in progress, few are likely to succeed and become dominate globally. The Superapp club will be a very small group. For these and the other reasons previously discussed, most organizations will not invest in creating a Superapp. They will, however, increasingly focus on how to exist in a world that is dominated by them.

The Superapp era is coming. It's already in China, and beginning its takeover throughout Asia. To understand how brands can exist and prosper in this new paradigm, companies can look to China for examples. Thousands of global brands have leveraged China's Superapps to enter China's marketplace with surprising success, as illustrated by the following use cases.

Hospitality - Starbucks

As we have seen, not everyone can make a Superapp. Of all the US retailers, Starbucks has been the most successful. The Starbucks App had phenomenal adoption rates and led the US mobile payment market for nearly a decade. When Starbucks considered its digital strategy in China, it was entering a very different market from those with which it had prior experience.

Unlike the western world, the Chinese market was saturated with newly developing Superapps. WeChat Pay and Alipay dominated the mobile payment sector and were becoming increasingly popular with users. Starbucks recognized that successfully realizing their China dreams meant finding a way to embrace the Superapps.

In 2016, Starbucks announced, "just as Starbucks cards are among the most gifted around the globe, we aspire to also become the most gifted brand digitally in China." After many discussions with WeChat and Tencent, they released a solution that would achieve that aspiration. Starbuck's "Say it with Starbucks" mini programs was a quick hit amongst Chinese. Furthermore, finally integrating with one of the mobile payment providers, WeChat Pay, saw a boost in Starbucks sales and enabled Starbucks entry into the modern Chinese market.

Background

Starbucks is a global cafe chain founded in Seattle in 1972. In 1999, Starbucks officially entered Mainland China with its first cafe in Beijing.

In 2016, as WeChat began discussing a potential partnership with Starbucks, the chain was flourishing in China. Starbucks had aggressive plans in the country and envisioned China as their largest growth market. Starbucks plan was to grow and consolidate. Starbucks already had more than 2,300 outlets in China. They set an aggressive expansion target to double their stores to a total of 5,000 stores by 2021. Starbucks was on track, opening a new store every 15 hours.

Half of Starbucks 2,300 stores at that point were only partially owned by Starbucks as licensed franchise stores. In 2016, Starbucks had already begun the process of buying back their share of the licensed stores, which would give Starbucks full operational control in Mainland China. The take-back was completed by mid-2017 with a 100% Starbucks ownership of their stores and brand. This provided more control over the Starbucks brand, which is their greatest asset, and was critical to maintain the high-quality standard of demands perfect execution that Starbucks requires.

However, when it came to the subject of digital payments, Starbucks was cocky, and had good reason to be. They had enjoyed surprising success with mobile payments in the US. In 2011, after a few pilots and testing, Starbucks had launched its own mobile payment app. As a traditional brick-and-mortar cafe-chain, technology solutions should not have been Starbucks' forte. However, its developed mobile app, which enabled a loyalty program and mobile payments for in-store purchases, was a surprising success. In 2013, 90% of mobile payments in the US were made at Starbucks, which became the envy of Silicon Valley. (Wohlsen, 2014)

In early 2015, Howard Schultz, President of Starbucks, trumpeted their continued success in mobile payments. "Today in the US alone, over 13 million customers were actively using our mobile apps. And we are now averaging more than 7 million mobile transactions in our stores each week - representing 16% of total tender. That's more than any other bricks-and-mortar retailer in the marketplace." Starbucks CFO Scott Maw would go as far as to say, "I guarantee in the US there is no one else even close, as far as the number of mobile payments."

Starbucks held the position of the most successful mobile payment app in the US for nearly a decade, before it was dethroned by Apple Pay in 2019. That a mobile payment app specific to only one retailer could maintain dominance for such a long period of time speaks volumes about the US market's mobile payment sector. In the US, generic mobile payment apps like Google Pay and Apple Pay have struggled to gain purchase, and mobile payments as a whole have still not become dominant.

China's mobile payment market was an entirely different beast. In China, mobile payments were a rapid success. By 2017, China's mobile payments totaled US$19 trillion, about 120 times greater than the United States' total of US$137 billion mobile payments market that same year. (iResearch, 2021)

When Starbucks and WeChat began their discussions in 2016, most major chain stores, including KFC and McDonalds, had integrated Alipay and/or WeChat Pay years earlier, while Starbucks had remained stoically wedded to its own business model and failed to integrate third-party mobile payment providers.

Opportunities and challenges

Starbucks goal of leveraging WeChat was clear: promote social gifting. Starbucks wanted to enable social digital gifting to allow customers to gift a cup of coffee with ease. Secondly and more pragmatically, Starbucks wanted marketing dollars to promote their brand and product in China.

Both WeChat and Alipay were hungry for a partnership with Starbucks. By 2016, the war for mobile payments dominance in China was raging between these two giants. Starbucks remained one of the last great players on the sidelines, failing to integrate either payment tool. Starbucks had revenues of around of US$2 billion in China, serving an average 6 million customers per week, with an average weekly transaction value of around US$6. Buying coffee was viewed as the perfect type of high-frequency, low-value transaction scenario that establishes a habit for payment users. Both Alipay and WeChat Pay were eager to win this hefty prize.

Like most partnerships, this 'tasty treat' would go to the

highest bidder, or the party that could provide the greatest value. Luckily, Starbucks' main objective was social gifting, and no one does social in China like WeChat and its parent Tencent. However, that simple fact didn't clinch the deal between Starbucks and WeChat. WeChat needed to offer something more.

Starbucks was in no rush; in fact, they seemed happy to delay. This was surprising, considering that Starbucks had lofty growth goals in China, and Chinese consumers had overwhelming embraced WeChat Pay and Alipay. Starbucks delaying tactic was due to their impending launch of their own mobile payment system through a Starbucks app specific to China in mid-2016. Starbucks believed their own mobile app would fare as successfully in China as it had in the US. However, Starbucks had enjoyed their US success in a vacuum, as few successful mobile payment providers existed in the US market.

The Chinese mobile payment market was different. It was 40 times larger than the US market. Secondly, unlike Americans, Chinese consumers had already developed a habit of using mobile payment providers WeChat Pay and Alipay. Prior success in the US market had caused Starbucks to miscalculate the situation in China.

Miscalculation is a common occurrence with international companies in China. Foreign companies underestimate just how unique China's market and consumer tastes have become, which is a costly mistake in the world's largest marketing environment.

In early 2016, Chinese people were already beginning to leave their wallets at home in favor of WeChat Pay and Alipay. At the time, I witnessed several instances where Starbucks customers didn't bring a wallet and were unable to pay with cash or card. Luckily, the baristas had a workaround: customers could directly transfer money to the baristas personal WeChat Pay account, who would then transfer payment to the cafe on the customer's behalf. The demand for WeChat Pay and Alipay was so great, it had created a gray market where baristas were using personal accounts to facilitate commerce.

To be fair, this type of gray market mobile payment transaction happened at many other locations. Many small shops across China had not yet integrated mobile payments. However, it was surprising was that Starbucks, a large and respected establishment, had misjudged how quickly digital payment had become ubiquitous. This laxity was detrimental to Starbucks goal for consistent, high-quality costumer experience, and threatened legal jeopardy to their operations in China.

Solution

After several months of discussions, Starbucks and WeChat agreed upon a partnership plan that included new digital solutions. The bulk of these solutions wouldn't launch until February 2017. But once the agreement was struck, there was no reason to delay enabling WeChat Pay. On December 7th, Tencent and Starbucks officially announced the partnership. The following day WeChat Pay was available at the cash register (commonly referred to as WeChat Pay offline) in all 2,500 Starbucks stores across Mainland China. Customers could place an order at a Starbucks, show their WeChat Pay QR code on their smartphone, let the barista scan it, and wait for their coffee. No more transferring money to friendly barista's WeChat Pay account when you forgot your wallet.

In the official partnership statement, Tencent and Starbucks promised to release a social gifting platform that "encourages everyday acts of kindness and appreciation among family and friends. Customers will be able to select from Starbucks-branded gifts and products and add a personalized message of love, of gratitude or to simply uplift someone's day. Recipients of these personal and simple acts of kindness can save their gifts and memories on their WeChat accounts and redeem their gift at Starbucks stores across China to enjoy the unparalleled Starbucks Experience." Two months later, they did exactly that: Starbucks released one of the first mini programs for social gifting called "Say it with Starbucks" ("用星说"). It allowed users to buy, customize, and gift a digital card that the recipient could use at a Starbucks store. First a user would buy and customize a gift card. Mini program's expanded functionality (as compared to a website) enabled an extensive amount of customization. A user could add a message, a photo, or a short video to the gift card. This way, the gift arrived with more context, and users could express emotions and heartfelt gratitude while gifting a cup (or more) of coffee.

The solution was localized for China. A user could give a gift card directly to a WeChat friend. When shared, the 'wrapper', the encasing of the link, was uniquely designed for WeChat. The gift card wrapper looked similar to a Chinese traditional Red Packet, but was green with Starbucks branding. Once the friend received the gift, it would be saved in their Cards and Offers. From there, the friend could easily access their gift card next time they visited a Starbucks.

This was the first-time WeChat had officially allowed a third-party to create their own version of the WeChat original digital Red Packet design. The idea here was to piggy-back on Chinese people's nature of gifting red packets, and guide it to a new habit of gifting items such as coffee or gift cards. It capitalized on WeChat's digital version of the Red Packet, which was the single-most important factor in WeChat Pay's success. If not done tastefully, a poor redesign of the WeChat Red Packet could cultivate user distrust in both the function and the app. If WeChat had not proceeded carefully, they could have killed their golden goose.

This partnership had many firsts beyond the customized WeChat Red Packet experience in chats. Secondly, this was one of the first Mini Programs released, just one month after the launch of mini programs. Third, this was the first, and probably the last quote Allen Zhang provided for a partnership between WeChat and another company: "The strategic cooperation between WeChat and Starbucks enables us to bring the unique Starbucks retail experience seamlessly to hundreds of millions of WeChat users in China. We are happy to be the partner of choice of Starbucks and look forward to deepening our connection to our users through the highest-quality services."

It was a rather general quote, nothing too flashy. But why did Allen Zhang choose to provide a quote for this particular partnership? Simply put, Allen loves Starbucks. Maybe it's just the coffee. But considering Allen's thoughtful nature, it's likely to be something more fundamental: Starbucks' uncompromising focus on user experience. For that matter, it's probably for similar reasons that Allen also loves Apple and Apple products.

Starbucks takes a customer-centric approach and has an obsession to provide the best possible experience to customers far beyond what lies in the cup they purchase. Starbucks ensures they have appropriate interior design and music to provide a great ambiance, and a very human touch in that baristas actually call customers by name. Allen appreciates a human touch and has said that a product manager or anyone who designs a user experience needs to have a big heart.

Because Allen loves Starbucks, and because, as mentioned earlier, WeChat needed something significant to bring to the negotiating table to lock down and commemorate the partnership, this occasion led to the final and greatest 'first-ever'. On its release, the Starbucks mini programs was listed in the prominent WeChat Wallet (later renamed simply WeChat

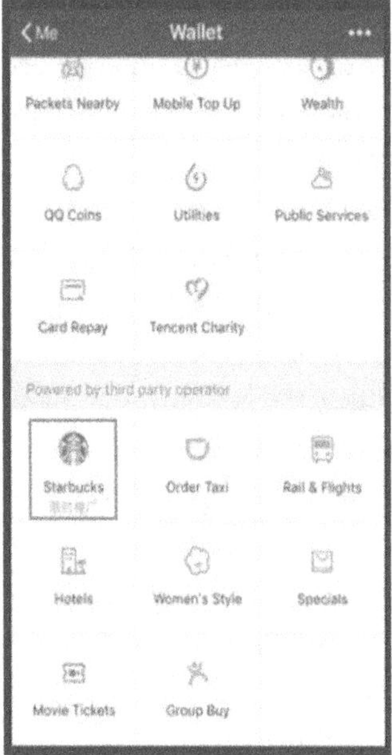

Figure 23: WeChat Wallet featuring Starbucks.

Starbucks was listed inside the coveted WeChat Wallet for several weeks (Chen Y. , 2017)

Pay). This was the first and only time a non-Tencent affiliated (invested or owned by Tencent) product or service has been listed in the WeChat Wallet.

WeChat Wallet was accessed dozens a time a day by the then 300 million payment users. Being listed in the WeChat Wallet was a huge source of traffic and every business owner's dream. The places in WeChat Wallet are commonly called, 九宫格, which translates roughly to "nine spaces," because it was originally a three-by-three square arrangement of links to more services supported by WeChat Pay. Since its creation the number of services has grown and the design has become multiple rows of three.

This major marketing contribution did more than just clinch the partnership with Starbucks. It was the token that moved

Starbucks stores to integrate WeChat Pay (and not Alipay) for nearly a year. This was a massive win in the battle for China's digital wallets.

Results

The quarter of the partnership release saw Starbucks China's (same-store) sales grow 7%, with an increase in transactions of 6%. This was largely attributed to the partnership with Tencent, which included the integration of WeChat Pay and the mini programs.

Customer adoption of WeChat Pay at Starbucks proceeded rapidly. Three months after Starbucks introduced the digital payment tool, WeChat Pay represented 30% of all the coffee chain's transactions in China. In the US, where Starbucks mobile payments were so successful, it took Starbucks eight years to reach the same saturation level. However, with the general trend of skyrocketing mobile payments, this adoption speed was commonplace in China.

The mini programs "Say it with Starbucks" was well-received by consumers. In the first seven weeks after the launch of the mini programs, over 1.2 million gifts were sent and over half were redeemed. Much of this was new revenue, as opposed to moving existing customers from one payment method to another. The gifts were helping Starbucks bring new customers into their stores.

At WeChat, the race to innovate new solutions to offer Starbucks in partnership discussions led to the creation of a new feature, Cards and Offers. This was a digital location to aggregate loyalty programs and promotional offers. Here a user's collection of frequent flyer miles and other loyalty cards, as well as discount coupons or gift cards could be found. To entice Starbucks, WeChat designed the loyalty program template with

"My Starbucks Rewards®" in mind. However, while the gift card solution was embraced by Starbucks, the rewards program was not. Starbucks did not want to lose control of their My Starbucks Rewards® program.

Tourism – CityExperience

Overview

In 2016, the war for mobile payment dominance was continuing to wage between Alipay and WeChat Pay. As discussed in digital payments, each side was frantically attempting to cover all possible payment scenarios and become the preferred tool within each scenario's vertical market.

Gradually, this war began to extend beyond China. A new payment scenario, cross-border payments, became the focus of this battle. In 2015, Chinese people spent US$200 billion a year while traveling overseas; it is predicted that 2025 will see that grow to US$450 billion. (Goldman Sachs, 2015) Countries and regions with large numbers of mainland Chinese consumers included Hong Kong, Taiwan, Japan, Korea, Thailand, USA, Australia, and more.

Chinese traveling overseas fell under my jurisdiction as WeChat's Director of Global Marketing and Partnerships. We decided to approach expansion by focusing on tourism boards because they were present everywhere at the national, state, and city levels. A partnership with a tourism board could be easily replicated in other locations. Furthermore, a single key individual was typically our contact within an organization; that single individual could provide access to the entire nation and/or city.

Opportunities offered by Tourism Boards

However, there was a slight mismatch in objectives between

WeChat and tourism boards. While WeChat is focused on bringing value to the user, it has no interest in where the user travels. In other words, tourism boards focus on bringing tourists to their location, while WeChat wants to improve the tourism experience by leveraging the WeChat app. In the end, WeChat's primary goal is always generation of user value. Despite this difference, we still saw opportunity for synergy.

Essentially, tourism boards are a location's advertising agency. Their job is to get people to visit the place they represent. What those people do once they visit is not usually within a tourism bureau's business scope. The exceptions are city tourism boards, which do have a more granular interest since specific activities and locations within the city attract increasing numbers of people.

As an example of tourism boards advertising, a fake reboot of the "Crocodile Dundee" movie aired as a commercial during the Super Bowl of 2018. This marketing 'stunt' created by a tourism board plucked nostalgic American heart strings for the Australian-American classic film series and enhanced Australia's image in the US. The targeted campaign, a hallmark of tourism boards, cost a record US$27 million. They call this activity "dream creation." Tourism boards make amazing and beautiful content to encourage people to set a goal of someday visiting this exotic place.

Another role of tourism boards is to provide data, such as number of visitors, visitor demographics, and so on to the government and the general public. Tourism New Zealand is especially good at providing clear and holistic visitor information— check it out for yourself at www.tourismnewzealand.com, then click on "Markets & Stats."

Yet, most tourism boards' data are surprisingly limited. They don't know much beyond a visitor's country of origin. Where did that person travel in-country? Why did they choose this place to visit? Why did they choose this time? How much did that individual spend? Tourism boards can't prove that their advertising dollars are bringing in people, nor can they provide clear ROI (Return on Investment). These data would be helpful to demonstrate the tourism board's value and judicious use of tax dollars.

For these reasons and more, tourism boards are beginning to look to tech companies for better solutions. They'd like to tag and follow tourists around their country. Even better, tourism boards would like to tag viewers of their campaigns and them follow them through the entire trip from going to the country to returning to their home. With this, tourism boards could clearly prove the economic benefit of their campaigns and provide valuable consumer insights to local tourism businesses.

Tourism boards objectives were marketing (awareness), sales (flight tickets and tourism activity booking), and data (knowing who does what). They had other secondary objectives, such as to improve the tourism experience, which was aligned with WeChat's goal. However, for tourism boards, especially higher-level ones at the national level covering multiple cities and even multiple states, gathering this information was outside their scope.

Opportunities for Chinese travelers

Understanding Chinese tourists helped to pinpoint areas for potential value generation. The idea was that WeChat would help tourism boards create solutions to market their locations while simultaneously improving the tourist experience.

To do this, we first noted a mega-trend: the number of traditional, large tourism groups of Chinese tourists had been shrinking, while a growing number of FIT (free independent travelers) were emerging. Young Chinese were opting out of notorious Chinese travel groups, and creating their own adventures. A digital solution should target the growing tech-savvy FIT segment.

Secondly, the two greatest challenges for overseas travel for Chinese people were communication (linguistic) issues and navigation issues, in that order of severity. Communication issues manifested themselves across many aspects of the trip. In planning a trip, Chinese tourists could only refer to information written in the Chinese language, which limited them to visiting places that were within the Chinese consciousness. Most Chinese FIT would find places to visit on Chinese blogs, design a trip based on the blog, and not deviate. Obviously, these too were limited to places where other Chinese tourists had visited or commonly visited.

Many tourist attractions lacked proper support for information in the Chinese language. This caused many Chinese tourists to miss valuable historical or cultural lessons. For example, on a recent trip to New Zealand, I visited a bird sanctuary. The prize specimens were half a dozen live birds called the Takahe, a dinosaur-looking flightless bird which, until recently, was believed to be extinct. While viewing these ancient marvels, I overheard a family of Chinese tourists mistake the Takahe for a chicken. As the information at the bird sanctuary was only provided in English and Maori, the family unfortunately missed out on understanding the significance of what was directly in front of them.

Navigation issues faced by Chinese tourists are an anomaly of the modern age. Navigation services for overseas travel are particularly absent. The most popular Chinese navigation apps, Baidu Maps and Gaode Maps, with 31.4 and 32.9 percent of the market share respectively (iiMedia, 2017), had no overseas content in 2016.[1] Baidu Maps only began adding minimal overseas content late in 2016 and Gaode Maps did not begin adding overseas support until 2020. Google Maps was blocked from Chinese users in China; it was also blocked while traveling if they used roaming data with a Mainland China SIM card. Even when Chinese tourists bought local SIM cards and could use Google Maps, they were frequently unaware that such a thing was available to them. Like most Google products, Google Maps does not advertise and depends on WoM (Word of Mouth) marketing, which is facilitated by the quality of its product. However, this doesn't work when Google Maps is outside of the Chinese consciousness.

What navigation tools were left to Chinese while traveling overseas? Bing Maps. If they used an iPhone, they had Apple Maps as well, but most only had Bing Maps. Even with my Seattle and Microsoft pride, I have to admit that Bing Maps lags well behind the competing Google Maps. It was no wonder most Chinese people felt more comfortable traveling with their tourist groups. The new FIT segment strictly adhered to consulting travel guides they read before travelling to Chinese blog sites.

Solution – CityExperience

Considering the interests of travelers, my team worked with tourism boards to create an open-source mini programs template called "CityExperience". Essentially, it was a virtual map and digital tour guide to a city. The product aimed to help Chinese travelers with navigation and communication. To expand the user base, we met with and encouraged tourism boards to use and improve on the original open-source design concept.

CityExperience was centered on a map. At the time, this

1 https://kknews.cc/tech/eoqq2jq.html

was the largest gap in digital services for Chinese travelers. Implementation would provide the most value to Chinese people. It meant that they wouldn't need to download a new map application, and would instead just scan a QR code to access the mini programs.

The CityExperience digital map was primarily focused on tourist-relevant information. Unlike Google Maps or Baidu Maps, which provide information for everyone, this map highlighted information most interesting to visiting tourists. These would include must-see tourist Points of Interest (POI), such as tourist attractions, famous restaurants, and bars, and more. Each POI included an audio file in-depth introduction. An independent traveler walking across the iconic London Tower Bridge could open the 'London CityExperience' in WeChat, click on the London Tower Bridge and listen to an introduction while their eyes were free to marvel at the architecture. They could then see what other attractions were in the immediate area and decide where to go next. This functionality basically turned a city into a museum with a guided audio tour.

Finally, the base design included a recommended tour route. A user could follow this route without any pre-planning, which was perfect for the last-minute traveler who ends up having an extra day in the city. A tourist visiting London would see a walking route that was officially recommended by the tourism board with detailed introductions to all tourist sites along the way. This ensured that visitors would see all the highlights along the route. Multiple tours covering multiple days or short tours for a few hours were provided, each subset by travel requirements such as walking vs. driving. In addition, tours could be organized by focus, e.g., fine arts, history, education, and so on.

Result

Tourism boards liked the idea and were eager to reach Chinese tourists in their own digital space. Dubai, Sydney, and London launched in late 2017, followed several months later by Singapore, Seattle, and Auckland with each bringing new, interesting features to the original design. In the end, dozens of cities worldwide would launch their own version of the program on WeChat.

The tourism boards had various launch events and marketing to increase interest and use. For example, Seattle covered SeaTac, its largest airport, and distributed table toppers to participating attractions and businesses across Seattle. Singapore placed QR codes on the free tourist maps you get at the airport, which have a circulation of about 3 million a year.

Nonetheless, the program ran into its fair share of problems. Higher-level tourism boards (nationwide versus city-level) struggled to execute at the micro-level in specific locales. National tourism boards had initially led the charge to create CityExperience mini programs for their major cities, but struggled to gain on-the-ground support from local businesses and government. A second issue was at the product level. Simply put, Chinese generally plan more than Westerners. CityExperience was most useful to the improvisor, the person who didn't plan everything in advance. It took advantage of mini programs' key benefit of being ephemeral and spontaneous. Most Chinese simply never needed it because they plan intentionally, so much they rarely get lost, nor do they feel they are missing anything important. In short, the product solves a problem that most Chinese don't yet have. However, as Chinese attitudes toward independent travel become more common, CityExperience will facilitate their adventures.

Attractions - Burj Khalifa

Overview

Learning from my experience with tourism boards, I realized that local players had more control of on-the-ground experience. This ensured they had greater ability and incentive to improve tourist experience. This led me to working with the tallest building the in the world, the Burj Khalifa in Dubai.

The Burj Khalifa was built by Emaar, a real estate development company. Emaar developed housing, office spaces, entertainment, restaurants, and shopping malls, including the Dubai Mall, which is the world's largest. They didn't just develop real estate, but created a lifestyle. Emaar is known for monumental scale and ultra-luxury design. Emaar, as the name suggests, is the Emirates Airlines equivalent of real estate, the real estate solution for sultans, royalty, and aristocrats.

The Burj Khalifa team

At 600,000 people a year, Chinese tourists were the largest demographic visiting the Burj Khalifa, and they were also the fastest growing segment. In 2016, the U.A.E. relaxed visa restrictions, offering Chinese nationals visa-on-arrival, which resulted in a major increase in Chinese tourists. This created an opportunity on which the Burj Khalifa team wanted to capitalize. Other Emaar tourist assets, such as boat rides on the Dubai Fountain, the Etihad Museum, VIP rooms in the Burj, etc., also wanted to take advantage of this positive trend and looked to Burj Khalifa for leadership and sales generation.

Simply put, Burj Khalifa's objectives were similar to any central tourist attraction: Increase the depth of direct engagement with visitors, increase sales, improve the visitor experience, increase cross-channel sales generation, and bring follow-on sales to other attractions.

Solution

In the end the Burj Khalifa team developed a mini program called Experience Burj Khalifa. The mini program enabled ticket sales, an audio guide, and shareable post cards. Users could browse and purchase tickets to a Burj Khalifa tour, along with several other surrounding attractions. Additionally, the mini program provided an audio guide in Mandarin for the Burj Khalifa tour, eliminating the need for clunky rental audio equipment commonly seen at museums. To make things more fun, WeChat and Burj Khalifa partnered to make themed digital post cards that enabled visitors to snap a photo, add official WeChat and Burj Khalifa stickers, and share with their friends.

Results

The partnership with WeChat and the launch of mini programs' Experience Burj Khalifa required a ceremony designed for Dubai. On the launch day, Burj Khalifa was covered in WeChat as it played a two-minute video celebrating the new solution. As the Burj Khalifa is the tallest building and boasts the largest LED screen in the world at 33,000 square meters, we had a ready-made video venue. At the end of the video, we displayed the partnership brands and the QR code for Burj Khalifa's mini programs. This last was likely another world record: largest QR code ever created.

Smaller versions of the two-minute show were displayed on more than 200 screens throughout Dubai, including the Dubai Mall and Burj Khalifa. While in the West, offline marketing is increasingly seen as outdated, the offline-to-online capability of WeChat – just scan a QR code with WeChat – makes offline marketing incredibly effective. Effectively, offline marketing became Dubai's brick-and-mortar businesses greatest asset in the digital age.

Figure 24: Burj Khalifa Mini Program Launch.

Possibly the world's largest QR code to date. (Burj Khalifa, 2019)

Entertainment - Merlin Entertainment

Overview

In 2018, Merlin Entertainment was the second largest visitor attractions operator worldwide with 67 million visitors per year. The largest operator, Disney parks, had around 157 million visitors a year. (TEA/AECOM, 2019) Unlike Disney, which has built an empire around the cohesive 'Disney' brand, Merlin locations are eclectic and customized with the Merlin brand hiding in the background. Locations range from quirky Madame Tussaud's wax museums to family-friendly Sea Life Aquariums, thematic Legolands, and singular iconic structures such as the London Eye. Most people know these locations but don't connect them to the 'Merlin' brand. This is analogous to the relationship between Tencent and WeChat, where most of the world has heard of 'WeChat', but have not heard of the parent company, Tencent.

Merlin Entertainment headquarters had identified Chinese tourists as their greatest growth opportunity and wanted to leverage WeChat to support their attractions. Merlin attractions were using third-party platforms such as ecommerce or travel platforms to sell their tickets and experiences, for which they paid a 10-25% platform fee. This prevented Merlin Entertainment from establishing a direct relationship with their customers.

To correct this, Merlin Entertainments wanted to create a presence on WeChat and sell tickets directly to tourists, cultivate relationships, and improve the overall experience at their attractions.

Solution

Merlin launched mini programs solutions for three tourist attractions, all of which had ecommerce functionality so that users could buy tickets in an overseas currency. The two larger attractions also included digital maps that provided the real-time location of the user. Using this data helped Chinese tourists navigate the larger attractions.

A few additional functions unique to each location were implemented. The most interesting was the gamification feature implemented at Sea Life in Bangkok. An educational game was created inside the interactive map feature. Visitors were quizzed on information about aquarium exhibits, and could even hunt for treasures. Visual progress through the game was indicated by a fish avatar. Initially, a visitor was a small clown fish; as questions were answered correctly, the avatar became an increasingly larger fish type, culminating as a shark at the top of the ocean food chain.

Merlin Entertainment used multiple mini programs for each location. At Sea Life, one Mini Program is an ecommerce platform, while a second is an interactive map with an educational game. The ecommerce mini programs required specific financial credentials. The interactive map and game mini programs could iterate and change without the need to modify any of the financial features. This specialization allowed for easier auditing credentials, and improved the user experience.

As Merlin Entertainments owns the brick-and-mortar location, they were able to leverage a strong offline marketing resource. SeaLife created large-scale posters to optimize Merlin exposure to foot traffic, which numbers in the millions in the surrounding shopping mall, Siam Paragon. Tourists could scan a large QR code on the posters to quickly gain access to the mini programs.

23

Conclusion

For several reasons explored in this book, the internet in China looks very different from the internet with which the rest of the world is familiar. Chinese people search on Baidu, buy goods and services on Alibaba's Taobao, and watch movies on Tencent Video. At the center of China's Internet is WeChat. First and foremost, this is where the people of China communicate, congregate, and share ideas. It is where they say "good night" to family and friends living in other cities. Over time, WeChat has grown beyond this core functionality.

Now Chinese people use WeChat for countless tasks, including to buy things directly from brands, pay for things in brick-and-mortar store, send money to friends, and buy a few bananas from a street vendor. WeChat's payment functionality has the primary catalyst for China's massive boom in mobile payments.

The advent of mini programs has enabled WeChat to transcend the confines of a regular app and become an operating environment, a self-contained ecosystem of mini apps. People play games with their friends; collaborate and work on documents; buy things; and perform a myriad of other activities via more than 3 million mini programs. Mini programs have made traditional apps in China all but obsolete.

With this combination of payments and mini apps on a platform, and a monopoly on social interaction as its core fabric, WeChat became the world's first Superapp. In China, people can accomplish virtually everything via WeChat. WeChat has made business models feasible that didn't make sense as apps, opening up new possibilities and innovations.

While WeChat has been innovating, entrepreneurs in the world have been taking notes. First, other Superapps popped up in China, notably from Alipay and Meituan. These and other apps began adding mini app features and synergized them with payment tools on large user communities. Now, outside of China, Superapps such as Gojek in Southeast Asia or Swiggy in India are beginning to take shape.

The Superapp era has just begun. Facebook's Mark Zuckerberg has been transparent about emulating WeChat's ecosystem with social messaging at the core, alongside Facebook's own payment utility, the in-progress Lira project. Soon, we will see Facebook or Messenger transcend to a state of Superapp-ness. In addition to Facebook, many other players, both large and small, are developing their own Superapp strategies that will become apparent in the next few years. We should expect to start seeing WeChat-like Superapps begin to appear and dominate in the West.

China's digital leaders will continue to innovate and have break-out innovations which, despite barriers, reverberate across the globe. Short video platforms like Bytedance's TikTok is the latest innovation; it has taken the world by storm. WeChat has created their own short-video functionality with a social-spin, called Channels, which is gradually gaining a strong user base. What will be the next innovation out of China? Will the West be quick enough to emulate and copy it before it becomes popular outside of China, or will we see another Chinese product like

TikTok go global?

While China's tech world learned from and copied the West with a deft, practiced hand, the West is just beginning to learn from and copy China. Historically, the West led in tech and had no need to copy another country's innovations, but clearly that is changing. To stay ahead of the pack, the tech-savvy should keep a close eye on China. While the West has been slow to emulate Superapps and ubiquitous digital payments, soon the West will catch up. During this process, expect to see a rise in Western emulators of China tech.

Today, technology remains one of the fastest developing and most tumultuous industries. Technology trends are ever-shifting and difficult to predict. Investors make and lose billions, for every big tech start-up success story, there are a thousand unsung failures. Despite this uncertainty, I can confidently make one prediction, the future of tech will have a surprising number of Chinese characteristics.

While the West remains the overall leader of tech, in a few critical categories, China has taken a tremendous lead. China's mobile payments has exploded, surpassing the US by a factor of nearly 100; the short-video platform TikTok gave the world something new to play on, and WeChat's model is ushering in a new era of Superapps. Yet, these innovations are coming from China's internet, a different internet than that of the rest of the world. The West will need to understand this unique internet to gain proficiency in these innovations and localize them to their own environments.

My hope is that this book helps to provide readers with this contextual understanding of China and its recent tech innovations. With this knowledge, the reader should be able to better understand the current digital climate and upcoming global trends, which are increasingly influenced by China.

Bibliography

Buchholz, K. (2021, April 28). *Meituan Holds Power over Chinese Food Delivery Market*. Retrieved from Statista: https://www.statista.com/chart/24743/chinese-food-delivery-market-share/

Burj Khalifa. (2019, April 25). *Youtube*. Retrieved from https://www.youtube.com/watch?v=8nE5lSG9zu8

CGTN. (2020, March 11). *China's total tourism revenue in 2019 reached 6.63 trillion yuan, up 11% year on year*. Retrieved from China Global Television Network: https://news.cgtn.com/news/2020-03-11/China-s-total-tourism-revenue-in-2019-reached-6-63-trillion-yuan-OLDZXQvVXG/index.html

Chao, E. (2017, February 1). Retrieved from FastCompany: https://www.fastcompany.com/3065255/china-wechat-tencent-red-envelopes-and-social-money

Chen, L., & Huet, E. (2015, September 27). *Uber wants to counquer the world but these companies are fighting back*. Retrieved from Forbes: https://www.forbes.com/sites/liyanchen/2015/09/09/uber-wants-to-conquer-the-world-but-these-companies-are-fighting-back-map/

Chen, M. F., & Tan, J. (2019, March 13). *Apple, WeChat Tussle Over Mini Programs*. Retrieved from Caixin Global: https://www.caixinglobal.com/2019-03-13/apple-wechat-tussle-over-how-to-divvy-up-mini-program-revenue-101392032.html

Chen, Y. (2017, Febuary 17). Retrieved from https://digiday.com/marketing/how-brands-use-wechat-wallet/

Cheung, M.-C. (2019, October 24). *China Mobile Payment Users 2019*. Retrieved from emarketer: https://www.emarketer.com/content/china-mobile-payment-users-2019

Church, Z. (2017, June 16). *MIT Sloan School*. Retrieved from https://mitsloan.mit.edu/ideas-made-to-matter/platform-strategy-explained

CNNIC. (2022, Feburary 18). *China Internet Network Information Center*. Retrieved from https://www.cnnic.com.cn/

Crews, C. W. (2001, April 2). On My Mind. *Forbes*. Retrieved December 14, 2021, from https://www.forbes.com/forbes/2001/0402/036

Dial, M. (2013, November 19). Retrieved from https://www.minterdial.com/2013/11/wechat-message-bottle/

EL. (2019, February 24). *Modernizing Millions of Mom-and-pop Stores in China – Alibaba's LST platform*. Retrieved from Harvard Business School: https://digital.hbs.edu/platform-digit/submission/modernizing-millions-of-mom-and-pop-stores-in-china-alibabas-lst-platform/

eMarketer. (2019, November 23). *Facial Recognition Payment Users in China, 2018-2022 (millions and % change)*. Retrieved from eMarketer: https://www.emarketer.com/chart/232537/facial-recognition-payment-users-china-2018-2022-millions-change

eMarketer. (2022, Feburary 21). *US Proximity Mobile Payment Users, by Platform (2018, 2019, 2021 reports)*. Retrieved from www.eMarketer.com

Facebook, Inc. (2020). *Facebook, Inc 2020 Annual Report*. Menlo Park: Facebook. Retrieved from https://investor.fb.com/financials/

Go Play Travel. (2020, March 27). Retrieved from https://bkk.com.tw/sealifebangkokoceanworld/

Goldman Sachs. (2015). *The Chinese Tourist Boom*. The Goldman

Sachs Group, Inc.

Goldmish, J., & Wu, T. (2008). *Who controls the Internet?* New York: Oxford University Press.

Gopalan, N. (2004, June 14). *Tencent Prices IPO at Top End of Range*. Retrieved from The Wall Street Journal: https://www.wsj.com/articles/SB108715183007335644

He, A. (2019, June 10). *Average Time Spent on Social Media Declines*. Retrieved from emarketer: https://www.emarketer.com/content/average-social-media-time-spent

Hofstede Insights. (2022, Feburary 18). *Hofstede Insights*. Retrieved December 15, 2021, from https://www.hofstede-insights.com/

Hong, K. (2013, January 13). *TheNextWeb*. Retrieved from TheNextWeb: https://thenextweb.com/news/chinese-messaging-app-wechat-takes-its-games-across-the-world-in-a-bid-to-become-a-social-platform

Hu, L. (2017). *Ma Huateng and Tencent: A Biography of One of China's Greatest Entrepreneurs*. LID Publishing.

iFanr. (2019, January 1). Retrieved from https://www.ifanr.com/1155523

iiMedia. (2017). *2017 Q1 China Smartphone Map App Market Share*. Shanghai: IIMedia.

International Monetary Fund. (2021, April 15). *World Economic Outlook Database*. Retrieved from https://www.imf.org/

iResearch. (2015, March 13). *China Third-party Mobile Payment GMV Quadruples*. Retrieved from http://www.iresearchchina.com/content/details7_18379.html

iResearch. (2017, July 11). *The GMV of China's Third-Party Mobile Payment Shot up 113.4% in Q1 2017*. Retrieved from http://www.iresearchchina.com/content/details7_34723.html

iResearch. (2021). *China's Third-Party Mobile Payment Market Data Report*. Shanghai: iResearch, Inc. Retrieved from https://report.iresearch.cn/wx/report.aspx?id=3785

Jacobs, H. (2018, June 27). *Chinese people don't care about privacy on the internet – here's why, according to a top professor in China.* Retrieved from Business Insider: https://www.businessinsider.com/why-china-chinese-people-dont-care-about-privacy-2018-6?r=US&IR=T

Jianshu. (2016, January 11). *From Foxmail to WeChat.* Retrieved from Jianshu: https://www.jianshu.com/p/a9a426cbf1bf

Kemp, S. (2021, October 21). *Hootsuite Blog.* Retrieved December 14, 2021, from https://blog.hootsuite.com/simon-kemp-social-media/

Kumar, R., Maktabi, T., & O'Brien, S. (2018, November 15). *2018 Findings from the Diary of Consumer Payment Choice.* Retrieved from Federal Reserve Bank of San Francsico: https://www.frbsf.org/cash/publications/fed-notes/2018/november/2018-findings-from-the-diary-of-consumer-payment-choice/

Lu, S. S. (2018, May 27). *WeChat Development History: The Incidental and Inevitable Successes of.* Retrieved from 36kr: https://36kr.com/p/1722545504257

Merriam Webster. (2022, Feburary 3). Retrieved from https://www.merriam-webster.com/dictionary/platform

Mozur, P., & Isaac, M. (2016, August 1). *Uber to Sell to Rival Didi Chuxing and Create New Business in China.* Retrieved from New York Times: https://www.nytimes.com/2016/08/02/business/dealbook/china-uber-didi-chuxing.html

Newzoo. (2014, March 10). *China's Tencent Takes #1 Spot in Global Games Market.* Retrieved from https://newzoo.com/insights/articles/chinas-tencent-takes-1-spot-global-games-marketfree-report/

Newzoo. (2021). *Newzoo Global Mobile Market Report 2021.* Newzoo. Retrieved from https://newzoo.com/insights/

trend-reports/newzoo-global-mobile-market-report-2020-free-version/

Pinduoduo Inc. (2021, December 16). Retrieved from Yahoo! Finance: https://finance.yahoo.com/quote/PDD/

Ponnappa, S. (2019, February 11). *What is a 'Super App'?* Retrieved from Gojek: https://www.gojek.io/blog/what-is-a-super-app

Purnell, N. (2017, September 22). *Alibaba and Tencent Set Fast Pace in Mobile Payments Race.* Retrieved December 15, 2021, from Wall Street Journal: https://www.wsj.com/articles/alibaba-and-tencent-set-fast-pace-in-mobile-payments-race-1506072602

PYMNTS. (2019, June 26). *Unattended Retail Stumbles In China, But Global Growth Continues.* Retrieved from Pymnts.com: https://www.pymnts.com/news/retail/2019/unattended-retail-stumbles-in-china-but-global-growth-continues/

Ruan, S., Wobbrock, J. O., Liou, K., Ng, A., & Landay, J. A. (2018, January 8). Comparing Speech and Keyboard Text Entry for Short Messages in Two Languages on Touchscreen Phones. New York, New York, USA: Association for Computing Machinery. Retrieved from https://doi.org/10.1145/3161187

Shaban, H. (2019, May 30). *The Sydney Morning Herald.* Retrieved from https://www.smh.com.au/business/companies/respect-is-a-two-way-street-uber-to-ban-passengers-with-low-ratings-20190530-p51smv.html

Shankar, V. (2018, November 10). *Forget Black Friday, Singles Day is the world's biggest shopping event.* Retrieved from Quartz: https://qz.com/1458107/forget-black-friday-singles-day-is-the-worlds-biggest-shopping-event/

Soho. (2021, January 28). Retrieved from https://www.sohu.com/a/447145374_355019

Sohu. (2022, January 25). Retrieved from https://www.sohu.

com/a/330498033_285010

TEA/AECOM. (2019). *2018 Theme Index and Museum Index: The Global Attractions Attendance Report.* (J. Rubin, Ed.) Retrieved December 17, 2021, from Themed Entertainment Association (TEA): https://www.aecom.com/wp-content/uploads/2019/05/Theme-Index-2018-4.pdf

Tencent, Inc. (2020). *Tencent, Inc 2020 Annual Report.* Shenzhen: Tencent, Inc. Retrieved from https://www.tencent.com/en-us/investors/financial-reports.html

Textor, C. (2021, August 9). *Market size of online food delivery service in China from 2011 to 2020.* Retrieved from Statista: https://www.statista.com/statistics/699310/china-sales-in-home-delivery/

The World Bank. (n.d.). *Individuals using the Internet (% of population) - China 2020.* Retrieved December 17, 2021, from The World Bank: https://data.worldbank.org/indicator/IT.NET.USER.ZS?locations=CN

VCG Photo. (2019, October 26). *CGTN.* Retrieved from https://news.cgtn.com/news/2019-10-26/Is-facial-recognition-the-future-of-payment-in-China--L6ZXsNh0VG/index.html

Wagner, K. (2019, April 29). *Facebook almost missed the mobile revolution. It can't afford to miss the next big thing.* Retrieved from Vox: https://www.vox.com/2019/4/29/18511534/facebook-mobile-phone-f8.

Wang, Xing. (2009, January 12). *A mysterious message millionaire.* China Daily. Retrieved from http://www.chinadaily.com.cn/business/2009-01/12/content_7388202.htm

Wang, Y., & Mainwaring, S. (April). Human-Currency Interaction: learning from virtual currency use in China. *SIGCHI Conference on Human Factors in Computing Systems,* (pp. 25-28). Chicago.

WeChat. (2013, August 5). *WeChat Version 5.0 Release.*

Retrieved from https://weixin.qq.com/cgi-bin/readtemplate?lang=zh_CN&t=weixin_faq_list&head=true

Wohlsen, M. (2014, November 3). *Forget Apple Pay. The Master of Mobile Payments Is Starbucks*. Retrieved from WIRED: https://www.wired.com/2014/11/forget-apple-pay-master-mobile-payments-starbucks/

World Bank. (2022, Feburary 18). Retrieved from https://datatopics.worldbank.org/world-development-indicators/

Yuan, L. (2018, May 7). *Mark Zuckerberg Wants Facebook to Emulate WeChat. Can It?* Retrieved from New York Times: https://www.nytimes.com/2019/03/07/technology/facebook-zuckerberg-wechat.html

Zhang, A. (2021, January 19). 2021 WeChat Open Class PRO. *Conference*. Guangzhou: Tencent.

Zheng, X. P., & Xu, J. X. (2013, November 18). *Deconstructing WeChat (Part 1): The Predicament of Being Born and Developed.* Retrieved from HuXiu: https://www.huxiu.com/article/23232.html

Zhihu. (2019, January 11). Retrieved from https://zhuanlan.zhihu.com/p/54571274

About the Author

Kevin Shimota is a leading expert on digital technology in China, having been a senior executive at WeChat with over a decade of experience in the industry. His ongoing work includes speaking and conducting workshops for premier global companies on current trends and innovations coming out of China and how they can be adapted and integrated into the global tech community. A graduate of the University of Washington, Kevin now lives in Sydney, Australia with his wife and dog.

CPSIA information can be obtained
at www.ICGtesting.com
Printed in the USA
BVHW031610270622
640741BV00012B/432

9 789888 769421